Jazz Women at the Keyboard

Jazz Women
at the Keyboard

by Mary Unterbrink

McFarland 1983

Jefferson, N.C., & London

Library of Congress Cataloguing-in-Publication Data

Unterbrink, Mary, 1937–
  Jazz women at the keyboard.

  Bibliography: p.
  Includes index.
  1. Pianists—United States—Biography. 2. Jazz
musicians—United States—Biography. 3. Women
musicians—United States—Biography. I. Title.
ML397.U57 1983   786'.092'2 [B]   83-756

ISBN 0-89950-074-9

Manufactured in the United States of America.

McFarland & Company, Inc., Publishers
  Box 611, Jefferson, North Carolina 28640

To Larry

Acknowledgments

I am grateful to Rosemary Jones for her generous guidance and encouragement throughout the writing of this book. I thank my family for continually supporting my writing endeavors, especially my husband, Larry, and my eldest son, Barry, who both contributed invaluable research assistance.

Many others contributed to the book through their interest and assistance: Marian McPartland; Peter O'Brien, S.J.; Curtis D. Jerde, curator, and Bruce Boyd Raeburn, librarian at the Jazz Archive, Tulane University, New Orleans; Allan Jaffe, Preservation Hall, New Orleans; Beth Howse, special collections librarian, Fisk University Library, Nashville, Tennessee; Carol Comer and Dianne Gregg, Kansas City Women's Jazz Festival; Cobi Narita, Universal Jazz Coalition; Rosetta Reitz, Rosetta Records; Department of Music Staff, Duke University, Durham, N.C.; Shel Freund, Louis Braille Foundation for Blind Musicians; Gillian B. Anderson, reference librarian, Music Division of the Library of Congress, Washington, D.C.; J. Martin Emerson, American Federation of Musicians, New York; Leonard Feather.

I am indebted to those who graciously shared their experiences and aspirations to make this book possible: Cleo Brown, Norma Teagarden, Marie Marcus, Marian McPartland, Barbara Carroll, Betty Hall Jones, Joanne Grauer, Barbara Sutton Curtis, Patricia Sea, Joyce Collins, June Derry, Lorna Michaelson, Nadine Jansen, Frances Campbell, Claudia Burson, Bonnie G. Fuqua, Iris Bell, Lovell Litton, Beth Brown, Nancy Marshall, Mary Jane Brown, Judy Strauss, Phyllis Fabry, Carol Flamm, Joanne Brackeen, Jane Jarvis, Molly MacMillan, Consuela Lee Moorehead, Nina Sheldon, Lee Shaw, Noreen Grey, Miranda Hentoff, Patti Bown, Isabelle Leymarie, Patti Wicks, Ann Johns Ruckert, Corky Hale, Jill McManus, Judy Powell, Barbara London, Marge Hilton, Ivy Black, Willis Scruggs, and Peter O'Brien, S.J.

Contents

Please see Index for individual names.

	Acknowledgments	vi
	Photographs	viii
	Introduction	1
I.	Beginnings of Jazz	5
II.	New Orleans	10
III.	Lil Hardin Armstrong	22
IV.	Mary Lou Williams	31
V.	Women at the Keyboard	52
VI.	52nd Street	65
VII.	West Coast Musicians	79
VIII.	Pianists of the Heartland	95
IX.	East Coast Pianists	118
X.	Present Progress, Future Expectations	166
	Bibliography	174
	Index	177

Photographs

Emma Barrett   17
Lil Hardin Armstrong   23
Mary Lou Williams   32
Cleo Brown   59
Norma Teagarden   62
Marie Marcus   66
Marian McPartland   69
Barbara Carroll   77
Betty Hall Jones   80
Joanne Grauer   82
Joyce Collins   89
Lorna Michaelson   96
Nadine Jansen   99
Frances Campbell   101
Iris Bell   106
Nancy Marshall   110
Judy Strauss   113
Joanne Brackeen   119
Jane Jarvis   122
Nina Sheldon   129
Lee Shaw   132
Noreen Grey   135
Patti Bown   138
Patti Wicks   144
Corky Hale   148
Jill McManus   151
Valerie Capers   154
Barbara London   159
Marge Hilton   162

Introduction

There are two authentic American art forms: the western and jazz. A western can be simply described as a novel or movie dealing with frontier life. But though volumes have been written in attempts to define jazz, it remains elusive to verbal description. One thing at least is evident — some individuals *need* to play jazz and millions more *need* to hear it.

Women have been pianists since the piano was invented in 1709, and women pianists have played jazz since its inception around 1900. Two decades earlier, in the 1880's, through parts of the South, particularly in the area around New Orleans, men and women singers and instrumentalists experimented with the 12-bar form of the folk tune. They flatted the third and seventh steps of the scale a quarter tone, adding an identifying element of melodic style from the Negro spirituals. Inserting irreverence and piety, humor and protest, they created the most durable predecessor of jazz, the blues.

The early blues performers, who were often minstrels, usually accompanied themselves on banjo or guitar. A little later on, pianists provided background music for the wailing blues singers of the era, often improvising on the harmonic sequence of the 12-bar chorus.

During the 1890's, ragtime, a music of vitality and complexity, was in the air. A combination of folk and minstrel music played in brisk 2/4 time, ragtime was popular in saloons, in bawdy houses, and as the accompaniment for cakewalk dances. Ragtime music was featured at the World Fairs in Chicago in 1893 and in St. Louis in 1904. Piano rolls for player pianos as well as sheet music of favorite rags were available. The syncopated rhythms and rich harmonies were contagious, inspiring listeners to dance. Controversy lasted for years over whether ragtime was a decadent inferior music or a welcome, authentic black-derived musical art form.

Ragtime, in essence, was a disciplined music. Its intricacies demanded superior instrumental technique of the popular ragtime pianists who were usually solo entertainers. Scott Joplin, the dominant composer of classic ragtime, possessed a genius for creatively working early folk rags into the confined structure of ragtime composition.

In 1894, a New Orleans segregation code resulted in Creoles moving into a district closer to the Negroes. This brought together the music of both groups — the Creoles who read music and the Negroes who did not. By the turn of the century the music later to be known as jazz emerged from a blend of Creole music, plaintive blues and work songs of Southern field hands, fusing ragtime and spirituals which were the black people's early songs of joy and sorrow.

The new music flourished in Storyville (a segregated tenderloin district set up in 1897 and named for the resolution's sponsor, Alderman Sidney Story) in the French Quarter of New Orleans. The same musicians who marched in street parades and performed at picnics also played in noisy cabarets and gambling houses near the brothels. Many of them entertained passengers on the riverboats churning the waters of the Mississippi, spreading their musical message as far north as St. Louis. Musicians needing work gathered at Exchange Alley in New Orleans. Anyone wishing to hire musicians to play for picnics or dances could find them there.

Colorful funeral processions were regular occurrences in New Orleans. The band led swaying mourners with brightly-colored umbrellas out to the cemetery with plodding dirges, then cut loose on the way back with lively renditions of "Didn't He Ramble" or "When the Saints Go Marchin' In." The mourners were joined by those along the way until the street was filled with spirited, twirling, clapping dancers.

The word "jazz" was first used as a verb around 1910 by listeners to encourage the musicians to play in a more lively, improvisational manner, telling them "to jazz it." Then it became an adjective, describing the highly originative music, and finally a noun identifying the spontaneous rhythmic music expressed in as many different ways as the individuals interpreting it.

Jazz, with an unvarying four-beats-to-the-bar rhythm, and a melodic style, allowed the performers to either play the theme or improvise variations on someone else's theme. Because jazz is a collective music, each performer's improvisation affected his fellow performers.

Keyboard stylists James P. Johnson, Art Tatum, Fats Waller and Fate Marable were among the first well-known inventive jazz pianists. Tatum, whose technique was second to none, was visited by Horowitz and Rachmaninoff who marvelled at his keyboard precision, similar to that required in performing classical music.

King Oliver, Sidney Bechet, Alphonse Picou, Jelly Roll Morton and Louis Armstrong all were Storyville performers before the district was closed in 1917. Out-of-work musicians headed for Chicago, and later California and New York, where they regrouped and continued to strive for improvisational perfection. Early recordings have preserved much of their earlier work.

In the 1920's another form of jazz known as the Kansas City style became widely popular throughout the South and Midwest. Large sectionalized bands traveled from town to town playing primarily for dances during the Swing Era.

Boisterous Chicago-style jazz followed, along with jumping boogie-woogie in the 1930's and controversial whirlwind bop of the 1940's. Soon to come would be cool jazz, West Coast, avant-garde with its intricate sounds and rhythms, and third stream (a hybrid of European classicism and Afro-American). These would be followed by Latin jazz, free jazz and fusion.

From its unpretentious beginnings nearly a century ago, jazz has become an art music, demanding cultural respectability and international appreciation. Many things to many people, the music is ever changing, taking the best of the old and adding it to the new, acquiring new audiences as it develops, leaving contented listeners along the way at different stages of its evolution. With several idioms flourishing concurrently, jazz can be heard in clubs, at the ballet or symphony or as part of a religious liturgy.

Throughout this century, women pianists and organists, through their inspiration and musical ability, have helped shape the music. They taught jazz greats and played alongside the finest jazz musicians. These women contributed greatly to the fledgling art form, many becoming prolific composers, orchestral arrangers and bandleaders. They persevered in spite of prejudice to actualize their musical concepts of a blossoming art form.

Lovie Austin was an accomplished blues pianist who played, composed and recorded with the early blues singers and bands. Lil Hardin Armstrong, a pretty, bright pianist with classical training, joined King Oliver at 17. She guided the career of the most well-known jazz musician in the world, Louis Armstrong, and composed much of the music their group, the Hot Five, recorded on "race" discs.

Mary Lou Williams played through all the eras of jazz, leaving a legacy of hundreds of compositions and numerous albums. To ensure the continuation of her music, she set up a foundation to provide scholarships and training for gifted children.

Gracious English-born Marian McPartland is an inspiration to untold women jazz pianists. She performs at clubs and festivals, hosts radio and television shows, teaches jazz to schoolchildren, writes extensively and finds time to personally answer all her mail, even when she's on the road.

Besides such familiar names as Hazel Scott, Barbara Carroll and the flamboyant Dorothy Donegan, scores of other women have dedicated themselves to performing jazz. Veteran Norma Teagarden, Valerie Capers and Marie Marcus are just a few who still promote and perform their music which is certain to undergo more changes through imaginative women like Joanne Brackeen and Carla Bley.

These women love jazz. The explosion of creative energy and their need to play ensures a permanent place for them in jazz and a solid future for a true American art form.

I

Beginnings of Jazz

Plantation owners in America in the nineteenth century recognized the beneficial results of the singing that accompanied the work of the slaves. Song leaders were sometimes assigned to lead the slaves in certain songs which broke the monotony and led them to accomplish their tasks faster. The songs of the slaves had repeated themes of faith, weariness, patience and optimism.

In the late 1800's, ex-slaves bought small organs, often paid for in weekly installments which continued for a lifetime. That organ was usually the only valuable item in the freed black man's modest cabin. The work songs and spirituals (which the slaves had learned in the master's church) were recreated on the instrument. It was their main source of family entertainment. Young members of the family quickly learned to play from the older ones.

In the years that followed, as many of the black people moved to the cities, their organs remained important household fixtures. Many great pianists learned to play on the home organ, among them W.C. Handy, Eubie Blake and Mary Lou Williams.

Usually it was the mother who taught the children to play, and dozens of jazz greats first learned the thrill of mastering the keyboard from their mothers or female music teachers. James P. Johnson, the famous "stride" pianist, first studied with his mother. Later he admitted that to develop a firm feeling for the keyboard, he practiced in the dark. When competing in "cutting" or "carving" contests against other pianists, he could easily defeat them by inserting complicated glissandos at the breaks.

Margaret Mitchell, a black church organist, first taught Eubie Blake to play. He caught on quickly, and before long shocked his mother by "raggin'" the hymns his teacher had assigned him.

"Mamie's Blues" was written by Jelly Roll Morton in memory of a woman pianist he often heard when he was young. When he visited his godmother, he could hear her neighbor singing and playing the blues all day long. Her neighbor was Mamie Desdoumes and she had only three fingers on her right hand. Yet she played melancholic chords with her right hand and rocking bass with her left to accompany her sad singing.

Count Basie's first teacher was his mother, as was Willie "The Lion" Smith's. Luckey Roberts studied with another black musician, Eloise Smith. Earl "Fatha" Hines watched his stepmother play the organ and imitated her by setting music on a chair and pretending to play. His first teacher was Emma D. Young.

Thomas "Fats" Waller came from a middle-class family which objected to his becoming a ragtime pianist. Adeline Lockett Waller played both the organ and piano. Thomas (later to become known as "Fats") was her youngest child. His father Edward was a pastor and his grandfather a well-known violinist. The boy learned to play at the age of six and within a few years was playing the organ at his father's church. He often visited the Lincoln Theatre in Harlem and sat behind Maizie Mullins as she played piano for the silent films. She let him slide under the brass rail and sit beside her. Soon he was playing along. Soon filling in when she was ill, later on, he was hired for the job.

Jack Teagarden, his sister Norma, and two brothers, Charlie and Clois, were all taught classical music by their mother. From the usual piano instruction books, they became familiar with the basics. Charlie took up the trumpet, Clois the drums, and Norma played violin through most of her school years, but later returned to the piano. At one time Jack and his mother were a featured attraction at a local theatre playing piano-trombone duets.

Daisy Kennedy Ellington was the most influential person in Duke Ellington's life. She came from a family that showed marked artistic ability, and she was quite a good pianist. When Daisy died of cancer in the 1930's Duke sank into a depression. His later four-part recording, "Reminiscing in Tempo," reflects the happiness in her life and the despair of her death that affected him so deeply.

Not much information is available about women jazz pioneers. Music historians recorded little of their contributions to the new music. But some available bits and pieces have been used to compile thumbnail sketches of some of the early women of the keyboard.

One of the first important women pianists who played the black people's music was Ella Sheppard. She was the director of the famous Fisk Jubilee Singers who made their first tour in 1871. In the first group of nine musicians, seven had been born in slavery. Later the group, then eleven members, toured Europe where they were well received.

Pianist/organist/vocalist Sippie Wallace was born November 1, 1898, and had two brothers who were professional musicians. Sippie first played the organ in the local Baptist church. Born in Houston, she later moved to New Orleans, then to Chicago where she made her first recording for Okeh in the 1920's. After extensive touring with the T.O.B.A. (Theatre Owners Booking Association), she moved to Detroit where she lived for many years. She continued to play and sing on tours, in churches and at festivals both at home and abroad. Sippie shared the program with Linda Hopkins and the Dick Hyman Classic Jazz Band at the North Sea Jazz Festival in Holland the summer of 1982.

At the turn of the century good ragtime pianists were found all through the South. One of the most famous Northern women raggers was known simply as "Ragtime Mame." She lived in Pittsburgh and played ragtime around 1905. First-rate women pianists also played ragtime in the wine rooms and Negro clubs in St. Louis. Among them were Gertrude "Sweety" Bell, Louella Anderson and Theodosia Hutchinson who performed in the area around 1915. Pearl Hutchison was a pianist for singer Ethel Waters. She passed on her musical knowledge to her daughter Dolly who later became a trumpet player in Irene Armstrong's band in the early 1930's.

Blues singers performed their music of pathos and humor in the deep rural South before the turn of the century. The first ones wandered from town to town, singing on street corners, in bars and in railroad stations. Accompanied by their battered guitars, they traveled by train, boat or wagons. The most famous of these was Blind Lemon Jefferson, whose work was fortunately preserved on recordings during the 1920's.

The "Classic" period of the blues followed, during which the great women blues singers made their mark. Their powerful voices and showmanship augmented the simple music and turned the manner of performing it into a fine art. These women came from the backwoods of Mississippi, Tennessee, Georgia and Texas. Gertrude "Ma" Rainey was the first of the great "classic" blues singers. She toured extensively with her own five piece band. Her protégé Bessie Smith became known as "Empress of the Blues." Bessie's rich contralto was familiar to audiences attending tent shows and vaudeville productions throughout the South and later in Chicago and New York.

Mamie Smith, along with Laura, Trixie and Clara Smith, were all competent blues singers, though no relation to Bessie. Sara Martin, Ida Cox, Lizzie Miles and Alberta Hunter were others. Bertha "Chippie" Hill was a dynamic vocalist, as was Maggie Jones and also Victoria Spivey, whose moaning style was typical of the Texas singers.

Margaret Johnson and Edmonia Henderson (whose "Dead Man Blues" and "Georgia Grind" were accompanied by Jelly Roll Morton) became vaudeville favorites.

Lovie Austin (Cora Calhoun), born in Tennessee in 1887, was probably the first woman pianist to accompany the early blues singers. She studied piano at Roger Williams University in Nashville and at Knoxville College. An accomplished blues pianist, Lovie played for Ida Cox, Ma Rainey, Chippie Hill and another blues singer of that time, Ethel Waters. Lovie made her first record with Ida Cox in 1923 for Paramount. She and her band, the Blues Serenaders (Tommy Ladnier on trumpet, Jimmy O'Bryant on clarinet), toured with Ma Rainey and others. They also provided background for the many recording sessions which featured those great singers. Record hits included "Steppin' on the Blues" and "Travelin' Blues," both in 1924 and "Mojo Blues," "Heebie Jeebies" and "Peepin' Blues" in 1925.

Edmonia Henderson became well known because of "Brown Skin Man." That disc lists the accompaniment of Lovie and her Blues Serenaders. Her band at times grew to six members as the recording, "Frog Tongue Stomp" (Chicago, April 1926), verifies.

Lovie composed and arranged music for many of the "race records" of the period. She and Alberta Hunter wrote the familiar "Nobody Knows You When You're Down and Out" and the "Down-Hearted Blues;" the latter was Bessie Smith's first recording in 1923. Lovie and Alberta Hunter also composed "Graveyard Blues" for Bessie and wrote "Gulf Coast Blues," which Clarence Smith recorded for Columbia Records. She also arranged vaudevillian String Bean's improvised tunes for the orchestra at the old Chicago Monogram Theatre.

Lovie worked in the pit band at the Monogram for twenty years and followed that with nine years at the Joyland Theatre. In 1946, after nearly twenty years away from the business, Chippie Hill recorded some songs for the Circle Label. Backing her were Lovie Austin on piano, Lee Collins on trumpet, John Lindsay on bass and Baby Dodds on drums. Chippie's comeback was successful and she once again toured, appearing at the Paris Jazz Festival in 1948.

During World War II, Lovie worked for two years as an inspector in a war plant. Then she toured with her own shows for a while, and in the late 1940's became pianist at Jimmy Payne's Dancing School. She and Alberta Hunter were again recorded in the early 1960's. Lovie was a pioneer at the piano, and her dependable musicality enhanced the performances of others more than it gained her fame. Her completeness as a performer, leader, composer and arranger made her the prototype of women seeking a life in music. She died in 1972.

Lil Henderson was another pianist who accompanied vocalists who sang the blues. She accompanied Ma Rainey on the recording of "Trust No Man," which was released in August of 1926. Alberta Simmons was a shout player who, along with Eubie Blake and James P. Johnson, entertained the wealthy in New York during the 1920's.

Auzie Dial spent a lifetime at the piano. Born in Tennessee in 1900, she first performed publicly in 1920. Two years later, she was leading her own band. They played for a radio show and clubs throughout the Midwest. Work with larger jazz bands like the Creole Jazz Band came along a few years later. The next 40 years were spent in solo performances in Minnesota. Then she retired, performing only at an occasional benefit.

The first woman to play on the Mississippi riverboats is believed to be Marge Creath, who was born in St. Louis in 1900. The riverboats helped to foster a "school" of jazz which funneled jazz into the northern cities. Charlie Creath, her brother, was the leader of a well-known band in St. Louis in the 1920's. Marge married jazz drummer Zutty Singleton, who died in 1976. Following her own recent death of a heart attack, friends of the couple paid her tribute during a musical funeral service held in New York.

II

New Orleans

The first jazz ensembles were marching brass bands in New Orleans, a city steeped in French, Spanish and African cultures. As the street bands gradually became dance bands, the piano was added. Historically, the New Orleans band pianist has usually been a woman who sometimes doubled as the vocalist. Mercedes Fields, Blanche Thomas, Wilhelmina Bart, Martha Boswell and Lottie Taylor all played piano in New Orleans during the early part of the century. Martha Boswell and her sisters later became a nationally known singing trio. Dolly Adams, who was born into a musical New Orleans family, worked with early jazz pioneers King Oliver and Louis Armstrong while still in her teens. She was a band leader at the Othello Theatre until she quit the music business to spend more time with her family. The pianist did not limit herself to Dixieland, but kept abreast of the advancements of jazz. Several years later, Dolly formed a band (which included her three sons) and was again active until the mid-1970's.

Edna Mitchell played ragtime with "Papa" Celestin and also in a four-piece combo led by Louis Armstrong in 1922 at Tom Anderson's saloon on Rampart Street. The other two musicians were concert violinist Paul Dominguez, Jr., and Edna's husband, drummer Albert Francis. Camilla Todd played with The Maple Leaf Orchestra during the early 1920's. Olivia Cook was a classically trained pianist who returned to jazz after a concert career seemed unlikely. Besides performing with orchestras, she led her own combo, "Lady Charlotte and Her Men of Rhythm" (formed in 1965), taught instrumental music at her studio and traveled extensively to perform and teach about jazz.

The 1960's experienced a resurgence of jazz, and New Orleans was once again a mecca for aficionados of the original art form. The most well-known place to go was Preservation Hall at 726 St. Peter Street in the heart of the bustling French Quarter, where sidewalk artists and street entertainers abounded. The structure was built in 1750 as a private mansion. Throughout the years, it served as a tavern (during the War of 1812), an apartment building and an art gallery. The proprietor of the art gallery used to invite musicians in to rehearse for recording sessions. In 1961, a visiting young couple from Philadelphia, Allan and Sandra Jaffe, were fascinated with the concept and took it over. They decided to live in the mansion and operate the hall as a business.

Preservation Hall, located just a short distance from the muddy waters of the Mississippi, afforded veteran jazz artists a place to play together the pure music they had helped invent. More than 20 bands with over 150 musicians from the Crescent City alternated nightly, their sweet harmonies and passionate rhythms spilling out onto the street to tempt passersby. The artists played for union scale, earning extra money by honoring requests for a dollar or two. "When the Saints Go Marchin' In" cost five dollars because the musicians were so tired of playing it!

The gray, weathered building, equipped with wooden benches and chairs, accommodated about 40 listeners, the overflow standing or sitting on the rickety wood floor. Though no dancing or liquor was allowed, the Jaffes never lacked customers wanting to hear tunes ranging from "in-the-alley blues" to throbbing stomps. They sold records of the performers and booked trips for them throughout the United States, Europe and the Orient. Some nights Allan Jaffe even sat in with his tuba.

Preservation Hall bands still play to capacity crowds both at home and in concert halls and festivals around the country. Over the years, jazz fans and young musicians from all over the world have made pilgrimages to Preservation Hall to hear musicians such as Billie Pierce, "Sweet Emma" Barrett and Jeanette Kimball play genuine American music that touches the heart.

Billie Pierce

School children, well-known entertainers, the young, the old, black and white, all followed the hearse down St. Claude Avenue to Corpus Christi Church. Led by the Olympia Brass Band playing "Just a Closer Walk with Thee," the procession came to a halt in front of a small modest dwelling where Billie and DeDe Pierce had lived for 30 years. Many of the mourners wept as the band struck up the

"Westlawn Dirge." Then they moved on to the crowded church where Bishop Harold Perry officiated at a requiem Mass for one of New Orleans' most loved musicians. Sweet Emma Barrett sang and Narvin Kimball accompanied the congregation on his banjo. After the services, the funeral procession wound its way to the St. Louis No. 2 Cemetery where Billie was buried next to DeDe, her partner in marriage and music for nearly 40 years. She had never recovered from the grief of losing him the year before.

Wilhelmina Madison Goodson was born in Marianna, Florida, on June 8, 1907, and soon moved to Pensacola. Her mother, father and six sisters all played the piano. Before she was old enough to speak coherently, she was picking out blues tunes and trying to sing lamenting lyrics about unrequited love. She never felt the need for lessons from that time on.

"Most all of my days I've been playing music," Billie told researcher William Russell in 1966. "I started playing the blues. My mother and father, you know, were very religious people. Me and my sisters would get around the piano and have a good time. Somebody watched out for Daddy and when he'd come, we'd break into 'What a Friend We Have in Jesus.' He never knew the difference."[1]

Ragtime jazz was plentiful around Pensacola, in halls during the winter and in waterfront parks in the summer. Kid Rena, Buddy Petit, "Papa" Celestin, Joe Jesse, George Douglas and other New Orleans bands often came to town. Billie and her sister Edna, forbidden by their father to attend the dances, would sneak out of the house after he was asleep.

Sadie, an older sister, was first to play piano with some of the bands, working mainly with Mack's Merrymakers, whose leader was from New Orleans. (She later gave up playing in public.) It wasn't long before Billie and Edna joined the Mighty Wiggle Carnival which toured through Florida, Georgia, Tennessee and Alabama. Billie, just 15, played the organ, sang and danced in the minstrel show. The first numbers she learned were "Pretty Baby," "The Bells Are Ringing for Me and My Gal," "I'm Forever Blowing Bubbles" and "Alcoholic Blues." Billie only worked with the show in Florida, playing Ocala, Orlando, Tallahassee, Jacksonville, Miami and Cedar Key.

Whenever the manager of the Belmont Theatre in Pensacola needed a piano player, he sent for one of the Goodson girls to fill in. That's how Billie came to accompany the great blues singer Bessie Smith, who influenced Billie's vocal style. The first songs they did together at the Belmont were "Gulf Coast Blues" and "Whoa, Tillie, Won't You Take Your Time." From there, Billie traveled with the black vaudeville headliner, returning home when Bessie's company left the state.

Billie next joined the Nighthawk Orchestra in Birmingham, Alabama. In 1929 the young woman went to New Orleans to temporarily replace Sadie in Buddy Petit's Band on the Lake Pontchartrain steamer Madisonville. When Sadie was able to resume working, Billie returned to Birmingham and began playing dates in Alabama and Florida, sometimes by herself at house parties and later with bands. She worked with Mack's Merrymakers, Joe Jesse's Orchestra and Joe People's band out of Orlando. Musicians in those days made good money around Century, Florida, where gambling, moonshine liquor and dancing abounded. Billie later recalled that two exceptionally fine female pianists playing in Florida at that time were Willie Woods and Florida Beck. Their playing style was similar to that of Billie's.

About a year after her initial trip to New Orleans, Billie returned. Her first job was with Alphonse Picou's five-piece band at the Rialto Nightclub and later at the Pig Pen and Absinthe House. In the meantime, trumpet player DeDe Pierce had replaced Buddy Petit on the steamer Madisonville. One night Sadie, who usually came by to take Billie home after work, sent DeDe in her place. Within three weeks, Billie and DeDe decided to get married.

DeDe (Joseph La Croix) Pierce was born in 1904 in New Orleans. No one in his family was musical. When he was 17, a cousin gave him an old trumpet which he began playing by ear. He took a few lessons from Kid Rena and then learned his "dots" (to read notes) from Paul Chaligny, a veteran musician who had once led the old Onward Brass Band during the late 1800's. With Chaligny, DeDe learned from the Otto Langey method book.[2]

The trumpet player was influenced by the New Orleans marching brass bands he heard with "Papa" Celestin, "Wooden Joe" Nicholas and Kid Rena, whom he later played with. Both Kid Rena and Buddy Petit gave DeDe their extra work, sending some of their musicians along with him on jobs. He also played on advertising wagons in New Orleans and with traveling bands in Mississippi, Alabama and Florida.

Billie and DeDe's wedding at St. Peter Claver Church in 1935 launched one of the most durable partnerships in American music. The newly married couple first toured with singer Ida Cox through Florida before returning to New Orleans where they played on Decatur Street. All the clubs there—the Popeye, the King Fish, Charlie Palooka, Corinne's, etc.—had three or four-piece bands and many had floor shows. If a misunderstanding occurred at one place, a musician would just cross the street and play at another club.

Bunkie, Louisiana, was the next place the Pierces worked. A New Orleans club owner hired them and two brothers, Ernest and Paul Moliere, to play at his newly opened Club Playtime on the highway in Bunkie. After a year or so, they returned to New Orleans for good, settling in at the "Old Folks' Home," Luthjen's Dance Hall at Almonaster and Marais streets. "I Got Rhythm" was one of the up-tempo tunes Billie played there for skit comedians, "Yeah Man" and "Pork Chops." The musicians made about a dollar and a half a night, plus tips for requests.

Billie and DeDe spent much of the next twenty years performing at Luthjen's. Usually accompanied by a drummer, they played and sang all types of requests in their distinctive style derived from Billie's classic blues background and DeDe's Creole heritage (evident in "Eh! La Bas," one of the charming songs in the Creole patois he made famous) and his early days with marching brass bands.

The 1950's were troublesome ones for the Pierces. DeDe was stricken with glaucoma and lost his eyesight. Billie had a stroke which left her paralyzed for months. She was determined to recover so she could devote herself to her husband's care. DeDe adjusted to his disability, and the couple made an astounding comeback during the jazz revival of the 1960's.

Billie's rough and ready style was first recorded on the American Music label, with DeDe on trumpet. They were also recorded on Riverside (RLP370) for the Living Legends series and for the albums "Billie and DeDe Pierce" and "DeDe Pierce and His New Orleans Stompers."

In 1962 they joined the union and began appearing at Preservation Hall, first in the trio format and later as part of a band. The couple's playful musical conversation on "Freight Train Blues" became a familiar part of many New Orleans festivities. Their happiness in performing together the music they loved was contagious, and they drew capacity crowds in New Orleans and on tours throughout the country. The blind trumpet player's clear syncopated notes and his wife's earthy piano playing aroused both internal and outward responses from their fans, who clapped and roared their approval.

They played in St. Louis, in Mexico City (with the Young Tuxedo Brass Band), in Minneapolis, at the Cotton Carnival in Memphis, at Duke University in North Carolina, and at Stanford University in California. They preferred to travel by bus and rented one equipped with eight beds for their tours which sometimes lasted 12 weeks. In Memphis, the Preservation Hall Jazz Band led by the Pierces was applauded by Metropolitan Opera stars who came by after the opera in the Amphitheater. Popular demand brought the Pierces back to Atlanta for three concerts within six weeks, and they were scheduled for an additional two weeks in San Francisco after all performances were sold out on the original booking.

In the late 1960's the band toured Europe, Japan and several Iron Curtain countries. In 1969 DeDe was the first recipient of the George Lewis Memorial Plaque. He was cited for being an inspiration to his fellow musicians by courageously dealing with his handicaps and continuing to contribute to jazz.

The 1970's brought more visits to college campuses, five consecutive annual appearances in the Great Performers Series at Lincoln Center in New York City and a guest spot on the Dick Cavett Show. The Pierces' original music was used on the soundtrack of Woody Allen's movie *Sleeper*. In the summer of 1973, nearly 25,000 people of all ages gathered in Stern Grove near San Francisco to listen to DeDe, Billie and the band. Fans sat on grassy hills surrounding the stage, sometimes jumping to their feet when the rhythms compelled them to dance.

DeDe became ill that fall and when he died in November of 1973, Billie was inconsolable. DeDe was given an elaborate traditional jazzman's funeral with several bands playing a musical tribute to one of their own, and then his body was interred in St. Louis No. 2. "My heart is gone," Billie told friends. With DeDe no longer by her side, she felt there was no reason to live. Her health quickly deteriorated until she had to be admitted to Sara Mayo Hospital where she died in October of 1974.

Emma Barrett

Born in New Orleans a few years before the turn of the 20th century, Emma Barrett was to become a jazz legend. She found fame and musical kinship even though she seldom left the city of her birth. Her costume never changed over the years — a bright red dress, red beanie, red slippers and red satin garters with bells which jingled when she tapped her feet in time to traditional New Orleans jazz. Partially paralyzed by a stroke in 1967, the ageless pianist nonetheless continued to play Dixieland at Preservation Hall into the 1980's.

Emma was a self-taught musician who'd been playing since she "had to sit on a cushion to reach the keyboard." In 1923 Oscar Celestin persuaded the girl's mother to allow Emma to join his band. "Papa"

Celestin and His Original Tuxedo Orchestra rose to fame, launching Emma's career. She later worked with other prominent bands under John Robichaux, Sidney Desvignes and Armand Piron. She also played on the streamers, "The Capitol" and "The Sidney," alongside Louis Armstrong and other future jazz greats.

The 1940's and 1950's were spent appearing mainly with four- or five-piece groups in crowded Bourbon Street clubs. In 1961 she formed her own band, Sweet Emma the Bell Gal and Her Dixieland Jazz Band. "I got my name from being so nice and trying to please everybody," she always claimed.

Her business card promised that Sweet Emma would "ring her bells" and "spank the ivories" for those who hired her band. Personnel included Percy Humphrey on trumpet, Willie Humphrey on clarinet, Jim Robinson on trombone, Narvin Kimball on banjo (replaced later by Emanuel Sayles) and Cie Frazier on drums.

The veteran all-stars were in demand to perform at Krewe parties during Mardi Gras, to entertain late diners and after-theatre patrons at the historic landmark, The Old Absinthe House, and to cheer up patients at Charity Hospital. They played for private parties, dances, colorful New Orleans funerals and at clubs in the French Quarter; they also participated in New Orleans Jazz Club concerts.

In the early 1960's, Riverside Records commissioned a recording expedition to the birthplace of jazz to capture the music of a fading generation of black jazz pioneers who had chosen not to leave home in search of fame. A recording van went through the city seeking out seasoned exponents of traditional jazz. A two-LP set titled "New Orleans: The Living Legend" (Riverside RLP 356/357) resulted. Musical treasures, including selections by Sweet Emma and Her Boys, were preserved for posterity.

During the recording session, the thin pianist, dressed in civilian clothes, felt uninspired to deliver her best work at the keyboard. While technicians and the other members of her band took a 45-minute break, Emma went home to change into her red dress, hat, garters and slippers. When she returned, the group got down to business and recorded ten Dixieland tunes.

Emma paid a high price for not trusting banks. In December 1961, her life savings, which she always carried in a shopping bag, was snatched from her on the street. Her fans collaborated with Olaf Lambert of the Royal Orleans to arrange a benefit concert for Emma. The hotel salon was packed with cheering, stomping admirers of the perennial musician. The following March, Emma was again robbed while walking near her home. A thug hit her on the head with a brick and

Sweet Emma Barrett. (Courtesy The Historic New Orleans Collection.)

escaped with over $1000 she was carrying. Not seriously injured, she was treated at the scene of the crime.

In October of 1964, Emma led Her Preservation Hall Jazz Band at the Tyrone Guthrie Theatre in Minneapolis, at the University of Minnesota and at the Golden Garter in St. Paul. The concert at the Guthrie was recorded and the album, *New Orleans' Sweet Emma and Her Preservation Hall Jazz Band* (vph / vps-2), has been available over the years at Preservation Hall, where the bare floors and sparse appointments don't matter to jazz fans. The musicians often spent much of their breaks between sets obligingly autographing newly purchased albums. Emma's signal for ending the break was a few bangs on the piano.

Recorded with Emma were Jim Robinson on trombone, Alcide "Slow Drag" Pavageau on bass, Percy Humphrey on trumpet, Willie Humphrey on clarinet, Emanuel Sayles on banjo, and Cie Frazier on drums. At that time, several of the musicians were in their seventies, but played with unbelievable vitality and expressiveness. Emma sang "I'm Alone Because I Love You" and the funeral hymn, "Closer Walk With Thee," and played the keyboard in her unique percussive style to the upbeat tunes, "Little Liza Jane" and "Clarinet Marmalade." Record producer Orrin Keepnews called Sweet Emma's group "far and away the best-organized jazz band now playing regularly in New Orleans."

Because of Emma's aversion to plane travel, other means of transportation had to be arranged for her when the band had out-of-town dates similar to those booked in Minnesota or the trip to California's Disneyland in 1965. At the latter engagement the group caused such a stir and their music was so well received that "Sweet Emma at Disneyland" was recorded by Southland.

Health problems plagued Emma in the mid-1960's. She suffered from a leg ailment, injured her foot when a heavy cake of ice accidently fell from her icebox and was bothered with a abscessed tooth. The staunch performer continued to play (sans garters) to rave reviews at clubs, at Jazz on Sunday Afternoon concerts, at Tulane University and at the Cotton Carnival in Memphis.

Early in 1967, Emma suffered a stroke and was paralyzed on her left side. Again her friends rallied around her, and the New Orleans newspapers kept readers informed about the pianist's recovery. The fifth annual Heart Fund Jazz Jamboree, a fund-raising program Emma had helped organize, was dedicated to the ailing jazz artist. Her return to the bandstand was realized the following year at the Heart Fund's sixth jamboree. Despite having to use only her right hand, the indomitable entertainer, in a new red dress, played for her adoring fans.

In the February 1969 issue of *Mademoiselle*, Emma was written up as a legend with 50 years of Bourbon Street status. A photo of her on her front porch with a ragtime piano enhanced the article. The following year, the pianist-singer brought down the house on opening night of the New Orleans Jazz and Heritage Festival. Performing with "Papa" Albert French and the Original Tuxedo Jazz Band, Emma sang her traditional "Jelly Roll" for an enthusiastic crowd.

Dixieland Hall, a 19th century townhouse-turned-jazz-hall, closed its doors in April of 1971. Economic conditions and a rise in the union pay scale for musicians were blamed for the decision to close. Emma had worked there the last two years of the ten the hall had been in business and was on hand to sing the final song.

Always evasive about her age, the colorful entertainer continued to appear around the city during the 1970's and early 1980's. She and her band played at the New Orleans Museum of Art in City Park, performed occasionally at Preservation Hall and made several television appearances. Emma never strayed far from home, but through her simple yet eloquent music, made a lasting impression on visitors who came to New Orleans, seeking to hear "real jazz."

When Emma died on January 28, 1983, it was revealed that she was 85 years old. Her last performance was 10 days before her death. She had told her son Richard Alexis she'd never stop playing.

"She's playing with all the greats, now," he said.

Jeanette Kimball

Jeanette Salvant Kimball was born in 1908 and raised in Pass Christian, Mississippi. As the only member of her family interested in music, she was encouraged to study the piano when she was seven years old. Jeanette belonged to the Catholic church and took part in the church music, as well as playing for school plays and social events through her elementary and high school years. Attending the same elementary school were the musical Handy brothers.

The girl's natural proclivity for music was nurtured and developed by her first teacher, Boston Conservatory-trained Anna Stewart, who charged fifty cents for three lessons a week. Jeanette later said she "lived at the piano" those early years, her diligence presenting a problem for her teacher who couldn't keep her supplied with new material. The first sheet music she learned was "My Gal Sal." Jeanette possessed improvisational skills from the beginning and taught a music class when she was only eleven!

Some serious musicians maintain that music students need a good foundation of written work before actually playing the instrument. That type of study was beneficial to her, as well as her aptitude in transposing. Jeanette always said that hers was a God-given talent.

Jeanette first heard band music when dance bands went through town on their advertising trucks. "Papa" Oscar Celestin was told about the talented adolescent who had piano pupils of her own and visited her at home to audition her for his band. Though she had never seen an orchestration, Jeanette played "Alabamy Bound" and other pieces of her sheet music with such dexterity and flair, she was asked to join "Papa" Celestin's Tuxedo Orchestra. The year was 1926.

The other members of the group besides Celestin on trumpet were Paul Barnes on alto sax, Sidney Carrere on tenor sax, John Marrero playing banjo, Simon Marrero on tuba, August Rousseau playing trombone and Abbey "Chinee" Foster on drums. Jeanette made her debut with the band on September 19, 1926, at the Roof Garden.

Joining the jazz band meant moving to New Orleans, where she stayed with a friend of her mother. "Papa" Celestin had to promise Jeanette's mother he'd be responsible for his young piano player. The group stayed together for over two years and was recorded several times by Columbia. Along with stock arrangements, they recorded "My Josephine," "Station Calls" and other compositions by the members of the orchestra.

When the band finally broke up, Celestin organized a 14-piece orchestra and insisted that Jeanette stay on as his pianist. She readily agreed and found working with the big band much more stimulating. Special arrangements with more complex and challenging piano parts written for her were used exclusively. She especially admired the composing abilities of pianist/arranger Walter "Fats" Pichon. Narvin Kimball, who later became her husband, played banjo with the group. Performing at balls and other society events in New Orleans and traveling throughout the South, Celestin's big band never lacked work. They often went directly from a daytime job to an evening engagement with barely time to eat.

Jeanette remained with Celestin until 1935, when she quit to devote more time to family life. The musician continued to play in New Orleans and adjacent parishes, both as a solo artist and with bands which didn't travel. Parenting and resuming her education took up much of the time previously spent teaching.

In 1953, she rejoined the band still under the leadership of Celestin, who died the following year (1954). Celestin's nephew, banjoist Albert (Papa) French, then took over the group. Jeanette's mastery of the keyboard was applauded at appearances both at home and abroad, including a command performance for President Eisenhower.

Throughout the 1960's and 1970's, the pianist was a Bourbon Street fixture, performing at Preservation Hall, the Presbytere, the Royal Orleans Hotel and Dixieland Hall. (In 1967, a new Kimball upright was donated to the establishment to replace the battered one Jeanette had been playing.) She usually worked with French's Orchestra, but occasionally performed solo. Her unique style and artistry was preserved on the album, "Albert (Papa) French at Tradition Hall"

(Second Line-0112), in the late 1970's before French's death. The faithful pianist stayed on with the band under the leadership of his sons.

Jeanette's bracing ragtime has changed little, still reflecting all the joy and fervor of the musician's first performances more than fifty years earlier. Through her efforts, traditional jazz as a living entity has been introduced to new generations all over the world.

[1]Elinor Kelly, *Commercial Appeal*, Memphis, Tennessee, May 13, 1966.
[2]Jazz archivist Richard B. Allen, October 7, 1959.

III

Lil Hardin Armstrong

"Miss Lil," as she liked to be called, was just five feet tall, slim and light-skinned with Oriental-looking features. She entered the world of jazz when very young, became an accomplished jazz pianist and played with many of the great pioneer bands. She was pragmatic about the business aspects of a musical career. Without her musical tutelage and advice, it is doubtful that the great trumpet player, Louis Armstrong, would have attained worldwide popularity as one of the greatest jazz musicians and goodwill ambassadors that ever lived.

Her father died when she was two years old. As a toddler growing up in Memphis, Tennessee, Lil played the family organ while her cousin worked the pedals. At the age of six she began taking music lessons from one of her school teachers and was playing at church and school a few years later. "One piece I especially remember was 'Onward, Christian Soldiers,' " she later said. "I might have known I was going to end up in jazz because I played 'Onward Christian Soldiers' with a definite beat! ... it was real funny, and the pastor used to look at me over his glasses."[1]

Lil's grandmother and mother both disapproved of jazz and wouldn't let the girl around anyone who played it. In 1917 Lil was allowed to buy her first sheet music. She learned to play "They Made It Twice as Nice as Paradise and Called It Dixieland" and "Alexander's Ragtime Band." At 15 Lil enrolled as a music major at Fisk University. Her mother and stepfather moved from Memphis to Chicago, so Lil went there in the summer of 1918 to spend her vacation from school. While visiting the Jones' Music Store on State Street, she asked the demonstrator if she could play the sheet music she intended to buy. When he heard her play, he offered her a job as demonstrator at three dollars a week. Over her mother's objections, Lil took the job. She was an asset to the business, and before long her wages were raised to eight dollars a week.

Lil Hardin Armstrong. (Courtesy Frank Driggs Collection.)

One day Jelly Roll Morton came in the store and sat down at the piano. Lil couldn't help staring at his long fingers. "In no time at all, he had the piano rockin' and he played so heavy," she said. "...the goose pimples were just stickin' out all over me...I was so thrilled...after that I played just as hard as I could, just like Jelly Roll did. Until this day I am still a heavy piano player."[2]

The music store owner also booked bands and one day brought the New Orleans Creole Jazz Band to town to play at a Chinese restaurant on the west side of town. The first piece they played was "Livery Stable Blues." That was the moment Lil abandoned the classics. The band was looking for a pianist and several male pianists had been heard before someone urged Lil to audition for the job. She later remembered her difficulty in understanding what was expected of her. "The band didn't play by music," she said. "When I asked, 'What key?' they didn't know what I was talking about. I was told 'When the leader gives two knocks, you start playing.' "[3]

After two knocks, she fell in with the band and played hard. She found she had an instinct for the Dixieland music and, after the audition, was asked to stay. Knowing what her mother would say about playing in dirty cabarets and saloons, Lil accepted the job without telling her parents. Three months went by before she was spotted by one of her mother's friends. Lil's mother was appalled, but Lil cried and begged her permission to continue. A compromise was worked out. Much to Lil's embarrassment, her mother would show up every night to take her home. "From nine to about ten minutes to one, I was the 'hot Miss Lil,' " she said. "Ten minutes to one, my mother would be standing at the door. 'Why don't you wait downstairs,' I'd say."[4]

The South Side of Chicago was already jumping with cabarets and piano players. The arrival of jazz bands livened it up all the more, and brought more musicians, black and white, to the area. In 1918 Joe "King" Oliver had left New Orleans for Chicago, joining a band which played at the Royal Gardens Cafe. He went over to the Dreamland where Lil was playing and asked her to work with him. She gave her two weeks' notice and started rehearsing with Oliver. By 1920 he was leading his own group at the crowded Dreamland Cafe where singers belted out songs without the aid of a microphone and went from table to table singing for tips. Oliver also played from after midnight until morning at the Pekin Cafe on State Street with five other musicians. Lil Hardin, then 18, was his pianist. The others were Johnny Dodds, Honore Dutrey, Ed Garland and Minor Hall, all from New Orleans.

Lil later described the band members as a sober group who drank very little, even though the liquor was always available. Dodds and Dutrey were thought to be serious and businesslike. Of King Oliver, she said, "He smoked cigars but he didn't drink." King Oliver's Creole Jazz Band was fast becoming known as the best band in Chicago, and Lil enjoyed the musical life and the money which she loved to spend on stylish clothes. They packed them in at places like the Lincoln Gardens, a huge bare room that held over six hundred people. Over the dance floor hung an enormous crystal ball which slowly turned, reflecting fragments of light on the dancers. The band performed on a platform with Lil's piano positioned in the center behind the horns. The crowds couldn't get enough of the hot band that played loud and fast, chorus after chorus, until the dancers were near exhaustion. Sometimes Lil would add a few flashy runs on her own, and King Oliver would scowl and inform her that the band already had a clarinet!

Around this time, Baby Dodds, whom Lil considered to be the playboy of the group, replaced Hall on drums and Bill Johnson became the new bass player. Oliver decided he wanted to add a second cornet and sent for Louis Armstrong, a young musician in New Orleans, who had first learned to play the cornet while confined in the Colored Waifs' Home. He had fired a pistol in the street to celebrate New Year's Eve and was arrested. After his release from the home, Louis had worked at odd jobs and played in honky-tonks, where he had been heard by the great Joe Oliver, who coached him and found him jobs. Louis was soon steadily employed in the red-light district and entered a tumultuous marriage with Daisy Parker.

When Oliver left for Chicago, Louis replaced him in the Kid Ory Band. Following his separation from Daisy, he worked on Mississippi excursion steamers where he improved his reading abilities. Louis never forgot Oliver's generosity. Years later, when he had traveled the world, worked in television and movies and capped off his mountain of million-record hits with "Hello, Dolly," he credited Oliver with being the greatest influence on his career.

In 1922 he received the message that altered the course of music. He often recalled reading that telegram as the happiest moment of his life. He said goodby to his mother and boarded a train for Chicago to join the King Oliver band. The band talked about "Little Louie" a great deal before his arrival, so Lil was not expecting the chubby young man who walked into the Lincoln Gardens where they were playing that night. "He weighed 226 pounds," she later said. "I was disappointed all around because I didn't like the way he was dressed. I didn't like his hairdo. He had bangs!"[5]

The word was out that Oliver had hired a young trumpet player from New Orleans, and musicians from all over town had come to hear him. Lil didn't know just how great the newcomer was until King Oliver confided in her one evening. He admitted that Louis could play better than he could. "But as long as I got him with me, he won't be able to get ahead of me. I'll still be king," Lil later remembered him saying.[6] The band was drawing not only crowds of dancers, but those who came to listen. Those who didn't look old enough to get in heard what they could from the sidewalk outside. Lil later said Louis and the others didn't realize they were making history and sometimes wondered why white musicians such as Paul Whiteman, Hoagy Carmichael and the legendary Bix Beiderbecke came by. "I didn't know their names," she said. "They used to talk to Louie, King Oliver and Johnny but they would never say anything to me. Never, never a word."[7]

Oliver and Louis played breaks together that astounded both the public and the visiting musicians. Instead of a few measures of solo improvisation, both men would jump up and execute complicated phrases in unison, each time different and each time perfect. It was later thought that Oliver either leaned over and hummed the next break to

Louis or that he would finger the valves to tip him off what to expect. Louis's phenomenal harmonic aptitude took it from there.

As Lil took more of an interest in Louis and his playing, he started spending more time with her, going for rides in her second-hand Hudson. Even though Lil was the only band member not from New Orleans, he found her manner of playing all four beats of a measure compatible with his idea of New Orleans jazz rhythm. New in town and uncertain about the future, Louis valued Lil's support. He began to listen to her ideas for his career, even agreeing to buy new clothes to replace the ill-fitting ones he had brought to Chicago. She shared with Louis her knowledge of classical music and spent many hours rehearsing with him. He later remarked, "Lil believed in me from the start...her believing in me meant a great deal."[8]

The band toured the Midwest in early 1923, then in the spring, took a train from Chicago to Richmond, Indiana. There they made jazz history at their first recording session at the Gennett Record Company studios. Many hours had been spent in rehearsal since Oliver had signed the recording contract for the band. Because they lacked a place to sleep in Richmond, the band traveled there in the morning, spent the day recording, and returned to Chicago that night. The only one not a bit nervous about the significant event was Lil Hardin. Her fellow musicians later admitted that only she remained calm through all the confusion.

In those days recording methods were primitive with the recording done acoustically. The music had to be played into a long tin horn which was connected at its narrow end to a steel needle that cut grooves in a revolving disc made of beeswax. The vibrating sounds were transformed onto the disc in the shape of wavy lines. When the wax disc, or original master, was completed, metal discs were electroplated: the "mother" or negative, the "master" or positive and another negative called the "stamper." The stampers were put into the record press with a "biscuit" of warm shellac which was pressed into a finished record.

Because of the precarious nature of the recording equipment, musicians often had to play a selection over and over to get a perfect original master. Any loud unexpected sound could make the needle jump the groove and ruin a wax disc. Jazz music especially had to be carefully controlled in order to complete a record without numerous retakes.

The King Oliver Creole Jazz Band, apprehensive but well prepared, was about to make musical history. But when they grouped around the bell of the big horn, there were problems. The two trumpets drowned out the rest of the band. King Oliver and Louis had to move back away from the horn, while Dodd's clarinet was pointed directly into it. Baby Dodd's bass drum couldn't be used. He had to get along with snares and a set of woodblocks. Then when Oliver and Louis began playing side by side as usual, it became evident that Oliver couldn't be heard. To achieve a balance, Louis was moved back even farther, away from the band. Lil later said that "he was at least 12 or 15 feet from us on the whole session."[9]

Under these adverse conditions, the band recorded 37 sides for four different labels that day. Definitely among the most important jazz discs in history, the rough recordings have documented the reputation of extraordinary musicians playing to achieve a perfect integration, resulting in a marvelous balance of sounds.

In February of 1924, once again disregarding her family's advice, Lil Hardin married Louis Armstrong. There had been disputes over money between Oliver and other members of the band, and when Lil discovered that Oliver was holding Louis's money for him, she decided that her husband should strike out on his own. King Oliver's solo on the band's recording of "Dippermouth Blues" became very popular. Louis wanted to learn that solo so he practiced it at home with Lil, but never was able to play it like Oliver. His disappointment made Lil more determined than ever that he get out of Oliver's shadow and play in his own style. "I told him I didn't want to be married to a second trumpet player. I wanted to be married to a first trumpet player."[10]

Lil stayed with Oliver after Louis quit. After being turned down by several band leaders, Louis landed a job as first trumpet with Ollie Powers' Band at the Dreamland. Later on, Lil left King Oliver when the band broke up. Eventually King Oliver formed a larger band, the Savannah Syncopators.

In September Lil and Louis left for New York where he joined the big dance band of Fletcher Henderson which was playing the Roseland Ballroom on Broadway. The decision marked an epoch in his long reign as top jazz musician in the world. He switched from cornet to trumpet, and his solos soared over the orchestrations. The Henderson Band was altogether different from King Oliver's. The music was arranged for the brass, reed and rhythm sections and the scores carefully followed. This was an opportunity for Louis to hone his musical skills. Soon after his opening, Lil returned to Chicago and her own career. Louis's trumpet playing had such an effect on Henderson's group that it not only influenced the individual musicians, but transformed the style of the band. He initiated the solo concept which would enjoy popularity for years to follow.

After 14 months with Henderson, he decided to return to the Dreamland in Chicago where Lil featured him with her band, Lil's Hot Shots. The contract promised good pay for the trumpet player. "The only statistic I remember is money," she said later when she told of Louis receiving an unprecedented 75 dollars a week. The Armstrongs then bought a house in Chicago and finally had a home of their own. Louis also doubled with Erskine Tate's band at the Vendome Theatre. There he was given the chance not only to play solo trumpet, but also to sing in his deep gravelly voice, something Henderson discouraged him from doing.

Lil told of Louis playing one number that ended on a high F and how people would come to two or three shows to see if he would miss it. He admitted to Lil that it worried him. What if he did miss high F? She told him to start practicing G's at home. "So then he'd be hitting G's at home all day," she laughed. "Psychologically I was right. If you can hit a G at home, you don't worry about an F at the theatre."[11]

Soon after, seeming to miss the relaxed intimacy of a New Orleans combo, he formed his own group, the Hot Five, with Lil, piano; Kid Ory, trombone; Johnny St. Cyr, banjo; Johnny Dodds, clarinet. They played at the Dreamland Cafe during 1925 and 1926 and recorded what would become required listening for aspiring jazz musicians. Louis continued to develop and perfect the solo. The band's own compositions were among the first released: Louis's "Gut Bucket Blues," Lil's "Jazz Lips" and Kid Ory's "Muskrat Ramble." Much of Louis's important work can be heard on these and other "race" records, for which Lil composed most of the music. Lil, who often doubled as pianist and vocalist, can be heard in duets with Louis in "You're Next" and other tunes. Her clear voice and sassy style provide perfect contrast with his. The Hot Five recorded nearly fifty sides and accompanied blues singers on dozens more.

The band's personnel changed often as did its name. Lil frequently took charge of booking the group, sometimes for Chicago dances that paid three or four dollars a night. Earl "Fatha" Hines once recalled that even the most fearless of men would have thought twice before entering some of the places Lil booked them.

The Hot Seven, Louis Armstrong and his Savoy Ballroom Five and other groups he fronted, all played great jazz and made hundreds of records. Some of these groups became merely accompanists for their gifted leader, and Lil was not content to play under those conditions.

Between 1926 and 1928, Lil played and recorded with the best musicians in the business. The New Orleans Wanderers recorded "Perdido Street Blues" and "Gatemouth" in Chicago, with Lil; George

Mitchell, cornet; Kid Ory, trombone; Johnny Dodds, clarinet; Johnny St. Cyr, banjo. She was also a member of trumpeter Freddie Keppard's small band in the Illinois area. "Freddie Keppard was a man-about-town," Lil recalled. "He drank quite a bit, a very good-looking fellow with lots of girls. And a very good trumpet player. Personally, I think he was better than King Oliver. I think he had a better tone. I liked him better."[12]

For a time, Lil studied at the Chicago College of Music, where she earned a teacher's certificate, and later at the New York College of Music where she received a post-graduate diploma. By 1931 Louis Armstrong had become very popular and things changed between him and Lil. As Louis spent more and more time on the road, she dropped out of his life. They separated in August of that year, but remained friends.

During the 1930's she led a 16-piece band with Jonah Jones playing first trumpet, organized an all-girl band and also formed an all-male band, which played for regular broadcasts. In 1936 Lil Armstrong and Her Swing Band did some recording in Chicago. Personnel included Joe Thomas, trumpet; Buster Bailey, clarinet; Chu Berry, tenor; Teddy Cole, piano; Huey Long, guitar; John Frazier, bass. One of the sides was "It's Murder," on which Lil sings the vocal in her bubbly voice. She also appeared alone in the revues, "Hot Chocolate" and "Shuffle Along," finally settling in New York for a few years where she worked as a house pianist for Decca Recording studios.

Though Lil and Louis remained friendly, after their divorce in 1938, there were disagreements over a suit by a music publishing company concerning the rights to certain tunes she wrote. Several of her 150 compositions were not protected; the losses ran into the thousands.

Lil spent the 1940's performing solo in Chicago, enjoying long residencies at the Tin Pan Alley Club, Garrick Stage Bar, Nob Hill Club, Mark Twain Lounge and others. In 1952 she left for Europe where she lived for four years, playing at Metro Jazz, the Alhambra and the Olympia Theatre in Paris. She appeared on television while abroad and played with most of the local jazz bands. During the late 1950's and 1960's she played in Chicago where she lived in the gray stone house which she and Louis had bought. Between engagements she continued to compose and to enjoy her hobbies of sewing and photography. Her occasional appearances in the East included Top of the Gate on Bleeker Street and Jimmy Ryan's. She played many benefits, such as the one sponsored by the Theatrical Cheer Club of Chicago, benefiting oldtime entertainers. Her youthful manner and spirited playing always endeared her to her audiences.

Though seemingly delicate, she was a talented spunky musician who believed in herself and others. From her early childhood, she never left the piano. On July 6, 1971, Louis "Satchmo" Armstrong died in New York City. Seven weeks later, on August 27, Lil participated in the Louis Armstrong Memorial Concert at the Civic Center Plaza in Chicago. The effervescent 73 year-old pianist was playing the "St. Louis Blues" when she suffered a fatal heart attack.

[1]Lil Armstrong, "Satchmo and Me," Riverside LP 12-120.

[2]Ibid.

[3]"Lil, The Forgotten Armstrong," *Ebony*, 14, (September 1965).

[4]Armstrong, "Satchmo and Me."

[5]*Ibid.*

[6]Martin T. Williams, *Jazz Masters of New Orleans* (New York: Macmillan & Co., 1967), p. 92.

[7]Armstrong, "Satchmo and Me."

[8]Rudi Blesh, *Combo USA, Eight Lives in Jazz* (Philadelphia, New York, London: Chilton Book Company, 1971).

[9]*Ibid.*

[10]Armstrong, "Satchmo and Me."

[11]*Ibid.*

[12]*Ibid.*

IV

Mary Lou Williams

"Mary Lou was only about three when she first played the piano, and from that time on, that's all she wanted to do." This is how Willis Scruggs, stepbrother of jazz great Mary Lou Williams, characterized her after her death in 1981.

Mary Lou Williams, the only major jazz artist who lived and played through all the eras of jazz, was often called "the history of jazz." Duke Ellington described her as "soul on soul" and praised her for being "perpetually contemporary" during a career which lasted more than half a century.[1] Whitney Balliett of *The New Yorker* called her "visionary."

She was respected and admired by her peers. She received Guggenheim Fellowships and honorary degrees from eight colleges and universities in recognition of her extraordinary life in music. In 1981 she was honored with the Trinity Award from Duke University where she spent her last four years as artist-in-residence, teaching and composing "God's music, the music that heals the soul."

Mary Lou Williams was born Mary Elfrieda Scruggs in Atlanta on May 8, 1910. She later became Mary Lou Winn and Mary Lou Burley, taking the names of her two stepfathers. She married musician John Williams in the 1920's, and though they later divorced, she kept his name the rest of her life.

Mary Lou's natural father disappeared when she was quite young, and her mother Virginia, remarried and moved to Pittsburgh, where she raised Mary Lou and eight other children in a poor section of the city. Virginia played the organ so the child was exposed early to music. Mary Lou liked to tell the story that her mother played the old pump organ while holding Mary Lou on her lap. One day the little girl reached up and quickly picked out a melody, surprising the woman so much that she dropped the girl and ran to tell the neighbors. "I must have sounded pretty good," Mary Lou later said of the incident.

Mary Lou Williams in 1941. (Photo by Rolland Shreves; courtesy Frank Driggs Collection.)

That was the beginning of her lifelong infatuation with music and countless hours each day at the piano. She first learned spirituals and ragtime from her mother, who never allowed a teacher to come near her. "She had studied and all she could do was read," Mary Lou said. "She couldn't improvise or play on her own at all."[2] Virginia arranged for professional musicians to come to the house and play for Mary Lou, who seemed to pick up the music by osmosis. The young prodigy was especially influenced by a piano player named Jack Howard. "He played so hard he almost broke the piano," she later remembered. "He had a strong left-handed ragtime style of that period. Later on I gained my first fame playing strong swinging left-handed piano."[3]

Fletcher Burley, her stepfather, was one of the three most important men in her life. He bought her a player piano with piano rolls of Jelly Roll Morton and James P. Johnson, a classically trained stride pianist who crossed over from ragtime to jazz. (Young Duke Ellington learned Johnson's splendid pieces by slowing down the piano rolls.) The purchase of a player piano meant a considerable outlay of money but from early on, Fletcher, in particular, seemed to accept and sustain Mary Lou's obsession with music, allowing the child to spend as many as 12 hours a day at the piano.

Fletcher Burley took Mary Lou to meeting places to play for his friends. When she was six, she made her professional debut with a union band playing at a picnic. "I couldn't read music at all," she said. "I just put it up on the stand and followed it by ear."[4] Burley would sneak her into nightclubs under his huge scratchy overcoat and arrange for her to play the piano. He'd put a dollar in a hat and then shame everyone else into adding money to the kitty. The patrons always got their money's worth when the tiny girl attacked the keyboard. And Burley always asked Mary Lou for his dollar back on the way home.

She played afternoons and evenings in their neighbors' homes, often bringing home quarters and half-dollars wrapped in a handkerchief. As her reputation grew throughout that part of Pittsburgh, her elementary school teachers tried to cultivate in their student an interest in classical music. Miss Milholland, the Lincoln School principal, took her to afternoon teas at Carnegie Tech, where Mary Lou played light classical pieces for the students and faculty. She also took the girl to the opera but Mary Lou wasn't influenced because she was so attracted to jazz. *Her* idols were Earl "Fatha" Hines and Jelly Roll Morton.

Known as "the little piano girl," she played at local talent shows in the East Liberty section of Pittsburgh. Once she was invited to play at a party given by the Mellons. A long shiny limousine was sent to pick up Mary Lou and a friend. Wearing starched Sunday dresses and white satin ribbons in their hair, the nervous girls were whisked away to the Mellon mansion. Mary Lou and her companion were met at the door and ushered through a foyer into a brightly lit room filled with guests. She was led to an enormous polished piano as her friend was seated nearby. The room became quiet and she began to play. The elegantly attired adults listened attentively and were astonished by the youngster's composure and extraordinary artistry. When Mary Lou finished playing, the chauffeur drove the girls back home where Mary Lou presented her mother with a check for one hundred dollars. "My mother was very upset," she later said, "and called to make sure there was no mistake."[5]

Mary Lou was impressed and influenced by the many musicians she heard in Pittsburgh. One woman made such an impact on her, she challenged herself to emulate her in later years. Her name was Lovie Austin, and Mary Lou first saw her one Saturday night when her brother-in-law Hugh Floyd took her to a T.O.B.A. theatre where all the Negro shows were booked.

Lovie was sitting in the pit of the theatre, working with the pit band. Her legs were crossed and she had a cigarette in her mouth. Mary Lou watched as the woman scribbled music for a coming act with her right hand while accompanying the band with her swinging left and conducting with her head. She never missed a beat. Mary Lou was so fascinated by the pianist, she was oblivious to the rest of the show. "I'm gonna do that," the eight-year-old told herself that night.[6] Later, while traveling and doing one-nighters with Andy Kirk's Twelve Clouds of Joy during the 1930's, she often played with her left hand and worked on orchestrations with her right while a cigarette burned in a nearby ashtray.

Her brother-in-law Hugh Floyd played a very important part in Mary Lou's exposure to music during her formative years. He took her along to theatres to hear Earl Hines and other pianists appearing in Pittsburgh. She and her friends loved going with him to dances where they could watch and listen.

When Ma Rainey, Queen of the Blues, came to a little theatre on Wiley Avenue, Mary Lou was taken to see her. The moaning, wailing blues singer with gold teeth was decked out with a diamond tiara, a necklace and flashy rings on both hands. Mary Lou later recalled thinking that Ma was one of the most bizarre sights she had seen as a child.

Musicians visiting the city would sometimes call on the young girl to join them in practice sessions. Members of Earl Hines' group and McKinney's Cotton Pickers often came by.

One morning a producer of a revue came to the house in East Liberty. He was looking for a pianist to fill in with his band, and a Western Union boy had given him Mary Lou's name. Climbing out of his big car, he inquired about her. When neighbors pointed out the tiny musician engrossed in a game of hopscotch, he scowled and grunted, "Oh, man. This a baby."[7]

Following her into the house, he reluctantly agreed to listen to her. Mary Lou ran her palms down her long skirt and began. First she played a haunting spiritual, slowly nodding her head to the plodding beat. Then she tore into a rousing "Who Stole the Lock Off The Henhouse Door?," a ragtime piece she had learned from her mother.

The producer's scowls turned to smiles of disbelief. He was amazed by the strength of the fragile looking girl and impressed by her sense of rhythm. He hummed the score and was delighted when she easily played it through. Naturally he offered her the job. Mary Lou played the show that night, and with her mother's permission and a girl friend to keep her company, went out on the road for the first time. She toured that summer with the vaudeville group Hottentots in a show titled "Hits and Bits." She was 13 years old.

She later told of that first summer on the road. "We toured carnivals and such, and it was an animal life. The worst kinds of people. I was a good student but I quit high school in my first year and went with another vaudeville group Seymour and Jeanette."[8] John Williams, a tall saxophonist with a generous smile, also played with the group's band. Mary Lou married him when she was 16, and they became a major act in white vaudeville along with Bill "Bojangles" Robinson, the dancer, who grudgingly had to admit about the attractive entertainer, "She sure can play."

Mary Lou and John went to New York in the mid-1920's and she sat in for a week with Duke Ellington's Washingtonians. The young musician was so impressed with the dapper Mr. Ellington, she referred to him for the rest of her life as the most elegant man she had ever met.

It was at this time that she met Fats Waller who was delighting crowds at the Lincoln Theatre movies where he played the organ. He was working on a new show on Seventh Avenue when Mary Lou was taken to see him. A jug of whisky within easy reach, Fats was composing, playing and breaking up the chorus girls with his clever patter. After the rehearsal, someone bet Fats that Mary Lou could play all the tunes he had just written. The bet was on. The young pianist, nervous in the presence of the musician she revered, managed to repeat all of his music. "He was knocked out," she said, "picking me up and throwing me in the air and roaring like a crazy man."[9]

A little later, when she visited Jelly Roll Morton, she didn't receive quite the same response. He was known to be very demanding both about his music and how it was played. Continually interrupting and criticizing her phrasing, he angered her. He wanted her to play "The Pearls" the way he played it. She later recorded the tune her way in 1938.

John Williams' group, the Syncopators, played around Memphis in 1927. Combos that played with a beat (jazz bands) were beginning to gain national attention. When John left to go play with T. Holder's band, Mary Lou assumed leadership and hired Jimmie Lunceford.

It was during this time that she also played solo engagements. While working in a roadhouse outside Memphis, a white patron came night after night to attentively hear the petite almond-eyed pianist. One evening the cook tipped her off that the man was interested in more than just her piano technique. He'd offered the cook 50 dollars to help him take Mary Lou to his place in Mississippi. When she learned of the kidnapping plot, the terrified girl ran to the restroom, locked the door and climbed out the window. She was too frightened to ever return for her pay.

Roland Mayfield, a man much older than Mary Lou, had taken an interest in her by this time. During the early part of her career, he would pick her up when she was stranded. He was a sporting type involved in gambling enterprises and had plenty of money. Perhaps he was in love with her. Generous with his advice and money, he insisted on buying her a new car every few years and remained a close friend until his death in the 1970's.

John sent for Mary Lou to join him in Kansas City after he had been with the Andy Kirk band (formerly T. Holder's) about six months. It was 1929 and they were enjoying a successful stay at the Pla-mor Ballroom. At first she drove one of the cars the band traveled in, sometimes sitting in to play a lively boogie-woogie number, "Froggy Bottom" to get the customers in a dancing mood. (Early on, musicians referred to "overhand bass," first used by Clarence "Pinetop" Smith in a number titled "Boogie Woogie," which became a popular dance record. After that, his type of overhand piano became known as "boogie.") Before long, the youthful musician with short-bobbed hair was filling in for regular pianist Marion Jackson, replacing him in 1930.

Mary Lou found Kansas City delightful. There was music everywhere, and she met and shared a camaraderie with musicians like Jack Teagarden and Ben Pollack. They took her to noisy after-hours clubs to hear still more music, never seeming to get enough of it.

Kansas City during Prohibition was a rough and wild town with many of the nightclubs run by politicians and gangsters. Musicians often found themselves employed by some pretty tough characters. One night at a dance where she was playing, a man's throat was cut during a scuffle in front of the stage. The cigar-chewing manager motioned for the band to continue playing so they did. The thugs were escorted out, the blood mopped up and the dancing went on without a pause.

Though Mary Lou did not drink much, she saw the inside of all the speakeasies on 12th and 18th streets. She made the rounds with her friends Lucille and Louise, assimilating the marvelous sounds coming from the bandstands. Her adventurous girlfriend Rosita went out of her way to look for excitement. The two of them were competitors in more than a few reckless drag racing events on the outskirts of town.

Mary Lou was learning to arrange music, but didn't know how to write down the chords she heard in her head. "Kirk helped me," she said, "and I learned."[10] She soon became the band's principal arranger, modeling herself after Don Redman of Fletcher Henderson's orchestra. She was first recorded in 1930 during what she thought was an audition. "Jack Kapp who owned Brunswick Records in Chicago, had heard about my playing and sent for me to come to Chicago so he could hear me play piano," she said. "Whenever I was asked to play piano for someone, I would compose new music while playing."[11] Unaware of being recorded, she played "Nite Life" which became her first solo record. From then on, at Kapp's insistence, she played on all recording dates for the Kirk band, most of them on the Decca label.

Andy Kirk's Twelve Clouds of Joy was one of the best bands to emerge from Kansas City. As part of the close-knit Kansas City school of jazz, Kirk's band played loose blues-based music with casual precision. During Mary Lou's tenure, the personnel changed very little, giving them a definite advantage over the mutable groups. Dick Wilson, Shorty Baker, Ted Donnelly, Ben Thigpen were all fine soloists, and Mary Lou's advanced arrangements accentuated their individual qualities. The Kirk band's recording, "The Lady Who Swings the Band," was a tribute to Mary Lou, their talented arranger and pianist. Other top local pianists were Roselle Claxton, Edith Williams and Count Basie. All through her life, whenever Mary Lou looked back on those years with Kirk's Twelve Clouds of Joy, she wistfully remembered what a happy time it was. "It was a good-looking band, an educated band," she often said. "We had such love for each other."[12]

Though she felt protected by the other musicians, she had a hard time of it at first. They were stranded in towns from New York to Colorado and often ended up not getting paid after a job. That predicament usually prompted one of the trumpet players to take out his horn and play the "Worried Blues" until they were laughing again.

One night in Atlanta, she was reunited with her stepbrother Willis. He and her sister Mamie had taken care of Mary Lou when she was small so her mother could work. They had not seen each other for twenty years, though he knew about her career with the famous Kirk band, whose recordings sold widely. "When I learned the Kirk band was coming to Atlanta, I bought tickets to see Mary Lou," he said. "After the engagement I took her around town, showing her our old neighborhood and the home place. Later on I went to New York and stayed with her and whenever she was in Atlanta, we got together. We became very close." The two most important women in her life were her married sister, Mamie Floyd, who was two years older, and her aunt, Anna Mae Riser. They were a threesome for decades. While visiting Pittsburgh, Mary Lou always stayed at Mamie's house.

When the band wasn't on the road, most of the musicians' time was spent around Kansas City. After-hours jam sessions often lasted halfway through the next day. "I'd stop at a session after work and they'd be doing Sweet Georgia Brown," she recalled. "I'd go home and take a bath and change my dress, and when I got back, they'd still be on Sweet Georgia Brown.' "[13]

When the band was in Cleveland, Mary Lou visited Art Tatum, who worked there when he wasn't in New York. Mary Lou later credited him with improving her technique. "Tatum taught me how to hit the notes, how to control them without using pedals," she said. "He showed me how to keep my fingers flat on the keys to get that clean tone."[14] The Tatum touch was evident in her playing, and throughout the rest of her career, she would not allow anyone to say anything detrimental about him or his playing.

The combination of Mary Lou's original material and strong swinging style greatly influenced the development of the music known as Kansas City Swing. Her best known works for the Kirk band included "Froggy Bottom," "Cloudy," "Mary's Idea," "Walkin' and Swingin'," and "Little Joe From Chicago," which she dedicated to booker Joe Glaser and Joe Louis. She later did charts for the Dorseys, Glen Gray, Cab Calloway and Jimmie Lunceford. She wrote for Louis Armstrong, and Benny Goodman who used her "Camel Hop" as the theme song for his radio show, "Camel Caravan of the Air." Her brilliant "Trumpet No End" was recorded by Duke Ellington in 1946 and featured his great trumpet section.

For a while everything she wrote was a hit. Though she was prolific in composing hits in the 1930's, she never received the remunerations she deserved. The melody line of "What's Your Story, Morning Glory?" was later taken in 1948 by Sonny Burke, and a middle section was added, along with new lyrics. "What's Your Story, Morning Glory?," as a new tune titled "Black Coffee," was then recorded by several other bands, but Mary Lou received no credit or payment.

Immersed in her music, she was often oblivious to the sometimes careless business dealings that went on. Once she received a new dress for a recording session, hardly sufficient payment for a musician of her stature. "When bad things happened to me, someone had to tell me," she said. "I'd be so lost in the music."[15]

After 12 years with The Clouds of Joy, something just wasn't right anymore. Mary Lou never seemed sure just why she felt she had to leave, but she knew she had to. She had already divorced John Williams by that time. "Little things upset me — untuned pianos, pianos with keys that didn't work. I began to feel my time was up, and one night in Washington, D.C., I just left. I was so upset when I left Kirk, I decided to leave music, and I went home to my sister Mamie's in Pittsburgh. But Art Blakey kept coming over to the house, pestering me to form a group."[16]

She finally did, first working a park in Cleveland, and then Kelly's Stable on 52nd Street in New York City. Harold "Shorty" Baker — he was her second husband — had left Kirk by this time and he went with her. Then John Hammond persuaded her to go to Cafe Society. Mary was happy on 52nd Street. "The street always reminded me of Kansas City," she said. "It was always a joy to play one of the clubs."[17] Her second marriage lasted barely a year. "I'd just fallen in love with the sound of his horn," she philosophized.[18]

Mary Lou and Baker toured with the Duke Ellington band for six months. Then she began appearing as a soloist, playing to capacity crowds at Cafe Society Uptown and Cafe Society Downtown. She acquired a large following of young admirers, many considering her the finest jazz pianist in the world. The only female musician equally employed and respected in the predominantly male world of jazz performers, she was at the forefront as the new music known as "bop" emerged.

Minton's on 118th Street was the spot to jam. As its predecessors, ragtime and jazz, this new music had no name. It was still in the embryonic stages. Players of various bands assembled to experiment with machine-gun tempos and extended chords, obsessed with creating a new music so complex, it would be impossible for others to imitate. Several of them were intent on getting a big band started to play the difficult music with everyone contributing to the arrangements. Mary Lou's apartment became a salon where ideas and encouragement were shared by the musicians creating the new sound.

"I loved them," she said. "Through association I learned a great deal about their chord changes and style of expression. The old blues took on a new look. The bop era blues chords added a great richness and more technique."[19]

The camaraderie with Thelonious Monk, Charlie Christian, Art Blakey, Kenny Clarke, Charlie Parker, Miles Davis and Dizzy Gillespie led to her becoming a consummate modern pianist and composer. Her originality in handling progressions and harmony greatly influenced the stylistic advancements of other jazz soloists. She wrote "Pretty

Eyed Baby," which became a pop hit for Frankie Laine and Jo Stafford. Milton Orent, a staff arranger at NBC, was a close friend of hers, and together they wrote "The Land of Oo Bla Dee" for Dizzy Gillespie and coarranged "Lonely Moments" and "Whistle Blues."

During the early 1940's Mary Lou's talents were shared in diverse ways. She donated her time to benefit the war effort and composed music for a revue, "The Victory Bandwagon," touring the nation as a member of the cast. 1944 brought her a citation from Paul Whiteman's NBC Philco Hall of Fame. In 1945 she started her own radio show, "The Mary Lou Williams Piano Workshop" on WNEW in New York. It was here she introduced her most ambitious work, "Zodiac Suite," performing her interpretation of each of the astrological signs, one weekly, for twelve weeks. She then scored the entire work for 18 instruments and presented it at Town Hall. Parts of the composition were played with the New York Philharmonic in Carnegie Hall the following year.

For a time, a photo of Mary Lou was on exhibit at the Museum of Modern Art. *Life* photographer Gjon Mili followed her around for months before getting just the shot he wanted in Boston. While visiting Pittsburgh, her brother-in-law told her about a young local pianist named Erroll Garner, whose technique and distinctive style impressed Mary Lou. She offered to teach him to read music as Andy Kirk had taught her, but Garner quickly lost interest. "I realized he was born with more than most musicians could accomplish in a lifetime," she said, later referring to him as the "Billie Holiday of the piano."[20]

RCA Victor released an album titled "Girls in Jazz" in 1946 which featured Mary Lou playing six sides with her "girl stars" — guitarist Mary Osborne, vibraharpist Margie Hyams, bass violist June Rotemberg, and drummer Rose Gottesman. She recorded another four sides for Continental with the same band. In 1948 she played with the Benny Goodman sextet and octet. She then worked at the Downbeat where she alternated with Billy Taylor, who admired her consistency to swing, whatever the context. "She'll take something pianissimo and swing just as hard as if it were double forte. She's one of the very few people who can do this," he said once during an interview with Marian McPartland.[21]

Mary Lou once made an attempt to see her father. It was in the early 1950's, and she needed a record of her birth to acquire a passport. When she arrived in Atlanta to visit him, he asked her if she had brought him anything. After angrily reproaching him for abandoning his family, she returned home in disillusionment.

She left for Europe soon after that on a goodwill tour. "I was sent to England to break the ban that prevented American musicians from playing in England or English musicians from playing here," she explained. "I was supposed to stay there for nine days and I wound up in Europe for over two years."[22] Europeans loved the pianist. She appeared in theatres and clubs in Denmark, Germany, Sweden, England and France. By this time Mary Lou could afford to buy good clothes and performed in expensive gowns, usually in her favorite color, navy blue. However, she became increasingly distracted and frustrated in trying to relate to people and cope with changing conditions in the jazz world, finally suffering an emotional breakdown. One night during a performance in Paris, she abruptly left the stage, calling a halt to her musical career for the second time.

Working constantly from 1922 to 1954, often for little money, had taken its toll. Appearing in public had its disadvantages. Musicians wanting handouts, indifferent audiences and declining working conditions bothered the sensitive pianist. She was 44 and the prospects of a husband and children seemed unlikely. Self–doubt and exhaustion paved the way to her emotional difficulties.

Mary Lou was also disenchanted with modern jazz, feeling the music was renouncing its roots and turning superficial. "Spiritual feeling is characteristic of good jazz," she said. "The moment a soloist's hand touches his instrument, ideas start to flow from the mind, through the heart, and out the fingertips. Therefore, if the mind stops, there are no ideas, just mechanical patterns. If the heart doesn't fulfill its role, there will be very little feeling or none at all."[23]

When the crisis occurred, Mary Lou did not become a recluse, as many believed. She used her recuperative power within to work her way out. After a brief rest at the country home of a friend in France, she returned to New York where she redirected her energies into helping others. 52nd Street had changed. The small combos were all playing cool jazz, displacing many musicians who were strictly swing era performers. The old haunts were being replaced by modern office buildings, and jazz musicians had no place to go. Many turned to Mary Lou for assistance. After selling several valuable possessions, she took troubled musicians into her New York apartment. She talked and prayed with them, cooked for them and helped them find work. She gathered another sister Grace and her four children around her, becoming so possessive of her nieces and nephews that it sometimes caused dissension between the two sisters.

Though she'd had no interest in religion from her early childhood, Mary Lou did carry a small Bible from the 1930's on. She considered different religions and joined Adam Powell's Church which she attended on Sundays. During the week she found solace in Our

Lady of Lourdes Catholic Church on 142nd Street. "I just sat there and meditated," she later recalled. "Music had left my head and I hardly remembered playing."[24] Music critic Barry Ulanov was interested in theology and belonged to a professional sodality. He put Mary Lou in touch with Father Anthony Woods, a Jesuit priest at St. Francis Xavier Church in New York City. Father Woods instructed her and her close friend Lorraine Gillespie (the wife of musician Dizzy Gillespie) in Roman Catholic doctrine. They both were baptized in 1957. "I converted to Catholicism for peace of mind," she told others. "I like the liturgy of the Mass and I like the peace and quiet in the church when I meditate. Being alone, I'm used to being in a peaceful environment."[25]

She led a rather ascetic life at this time, devoting time to prayer and meditation. It was during this period that she conceived an idea to help musicians with drug or alcohol problems. To get the Bel Canto Foundation started, she gave a benefit concert at Carnegie Hall, but expenses cancelled out any profit.

Soon after that, she found a place on East 29th Street in New York City near Bellevue Hospital, which she fixed up into the first of two thrift shops. Word of her new venture spread, and she was soon receiving expensive clothes and household items from Duke Ellington, Louis Armstrong, the Gillespies and others. Collecting and sorting donations, waiting on customers, and keeping the books kept Mary Lou busy all day long. Evenings she often visited the musicians seeking rehabilitation at Bellevue.

At this time spiritual advisors convinced her that no one was playing true jazz anymore and that she should return to her music. "They made me feel I could help others through my music," she said.[26] Close friend Dizzy Gillespie invited her to perform with him at the Newport Jazz Festival in 1957. She accepted his offer and started playing club dates again. Mary Records, her own label, was founded, with part of all proceeds going to Bel Canto. She went on to initiate a campaign to persuade radio stations to program more jazz and worked to establish the annual Pittsburgh Jazz Festival. She appeared at the Composer, the Embers, Hickory House and others.

One day Mary Lou played a new work for her friend Lorraine Gillespie. A musical satire on new trends in avant-garde music she felt threatened jazz, Lorraine like it, "A Fungus Amungus."

Her first major religious work was "Black Christ of the Andes," a modern jazz hymn in honor of St. Martin de Porres, the black South American saint. The recently canonized St. Martin was the son of a Spanish nobleman and a Negro slave who lived during the 17th century. He spent his entire life helping the poor in Lima, Peru.

The haunting composition with complex harmonization, written in ballad form with lyrics by Father Anthony Woods, was performed by Mary Lou at Philharmonic Hall. This marked the first time jazz was used for sacred purposes.

While at the Hickory House in New York City, Mary Lou was visited by a young Jesuit seminarian named Peter O'Brien. He had read about her religious music in *Time* and wanted to meet her. "That initial experience changed my life and pointed it in a new direction," he said. Talking with Mary Lou between sets, he learned of Charlie Parker, Art Tatum, Dizzy Gillespie and other artists who created America's unique art form, jazz. "She talked quietly and eloquently about the black man's heritage in America," he said. "She had returned to playing publicly because so many of the younger musicians seemed to be unaware of the rich musical heritage that had been created. The music was in danger of being lost."

O'Brien listened to her beautiful music filled with soulful feeling as often as he could. A unique and important relationship developed.

He was avidly interested in helping Mary Lou spread the message of her music and scheduled appearances for her. She appeared at lecture-demonstrations, black history classes, grade school assemblies and churches. Mary Lou still seemed withdrawn and uncertain at times. Reticent while performing at the Hickory House, she sometimes would spend her time between sets in the coat room. Once back at the piano, though, she conveyed her message with exceptional taste and perception. "She was very sensitive, but very tough too," O'Brien said. "She was smart and in control. She got the respect she deserved only because her talent demanded it."

Mary Lou couldn't stand to be kidded about her music and admitted that during her days with the Kirk band, the men made her angry when they fooled around with her music. Because she had perfect pitch, their ill-played notes offended her ear. She'd snatch her music away from them and go home crying.

Mary Lou knew the sordid side of show business and educated her young friend. "She warned me of evils I didn't know existed," he said. "At the London House in Chicago, a sniffling white girl was hanging around, and asking to see Mary. I didn't know what was going on, but Mary Lou knew the girl was a heroin addict, and took time to try to help her. She later told me to never give addicts very much money at one time because there was the danger they would use it on drugs and O.D."

After the hymns, extended religious works followed, the first titled simply "Mass," written while teaching at Seton High School in

Pittsburgh. It was performed in a liturgy celebrated by John Cardinal
Wright, the Bishop of Pittsburgh, at St. Paul's Cathedral. In 1967 she
gave a concert at Carnegie Hall. "Praise the Lord in Many Voices" included "Thank You Jesus," "The Lord's Prayer" and "Praise the Lord," a
culmination of her religious fervor and superior musical artistry. She
was to write two more complete Masses: "Mass for the Lenten Season,"
presented on seven consecutive Sundays at the Church of St. Thomas
the Apostle in New York City and "Music for Peace," performed for the
first time in 1969 at a service honoring Tom Mboya, the assassinated
Kenyan leader. Commissioned by the Vatican, it became known as
"Mary Lou's Mass" when it was rescored for a series of dances used by
the Alvin Ailey City Center Dance Theatre in New York and on tour in
1971-72. Clive Barnes, New York Times dance critic, called "Mary
Lou's Mass," "Strong and joyful music, with a spirit that cuts across all
religious boundaries to provide a celebration of man, God and peace."
"Mary Lou's Mass" was to become celebrated all over the world in concert form, as music for dance and in liturgical celebrations in many
churches, including Church of the Gesu in Rome and St. Patrick's
Cathedral in New York City, where jazz had never before been heard.

O'Brien juggled his studies and volunteered managerial duties to
Mary Lou. After his ordination in 1970, he received permission to continue assisting her. She played for 18 weeks at the Cookery in Greenwich Village, initiating a series of annual engagements for several years
to come. "I spent one summer with a city parish, and the following at a
hospital in Harlem, so there was no conflict," he said. "By this time my
superiors were accustomed to our arrangement. They were aware of
Mary Lou's conversion and the publicity her Mass was getting." The
pastor of the Park Avenue parish where he was assigned agreed to let
him travel, as long as he caught up on the piles of work on his desk
when he returned from out-of-town engagements. "Mary Lou had
never had a manager during all her years as a performer. She would
not take the chance of losing control by signing with an agent who
would tell her when and where to play," he said. "We combined
religion and music. Often she would be fussing about an untuned piano
at the last minute in a crowded hall while I was trying to mentally
prepare myself to celebrate the Mass."

"Mary Lou worked harder during the last ten years of her life
than she ever did before," he said. "She worked at least ten months a
year and was composing besides." Her compositions number over 350.
The Masses were often performed at different churches and campuses.
These were preceded by rehearsals with the local choirs and bands,
who were performing the music for the first time. Mary Lou produced

several records on her own label, Mary Records, and did one solo album for Chiaroscuro Records, "From the Heart," and a duo, "Live at the Cookery." The first presented 11 original piano solos, six of them written especially for the album. The second was a live recording of Mary Lou (with Brian Torff on bass) during her three month run at Barney Josephson's Cookery. One of the original compositions was "Blues for Peter," a contemplative musical tribute to Father O'Brien.

Mary Lou's fear of flying caused her to turn down lucrative engagements she otherwise would have played. She toured Europe to enthusiastic audiences in 1968 and 1969. She was pleased with her reception, but when George Wein later wanted her to go to Germany, she refused. She turned down very good pay for a 45 minute set because she would have had to go by plane. "Mary Lou loved buses and trains," Father O'Brien said. "She was so happy on long bus rides. She'd settle back and enjoy the trip." Train travel was especially appealing to her. Never getting restless, she chatted and played cards as the train clicked along. Mary Lou was frequently recognized by a waiter in the swaying dining car or by one of the stewards. She was relaxed and contented among the train's personnel, who were often third and fourth generation blacks in those jobs." Because of pastoral commitments, Father O'Brien sometimes flew to California to meet Mary Lou as she cheerfully said goodby to her traveling companions while getting off a cross-country train.

On one trip to California, a publicist for Norman Granz knew of a hypnotist who would treat Mary Lou's fear of flying. She agreed to let him make an appointment for a session with him. On the day of the appointment, Mary Lou insisted on going in alone. Father O'Brien walked up and down the sidewalk outside the building while she underwent hypnosis. "Unfortunately, no real improvement resulted from it," he said.

Mary Lou played college concerts, club engagements, on radio and TV shows, and at jazz festivals through the early 1970's. She felt that jazz had a good chance of surviving if enough young people could hear it, so spent three to five days on different New York campuses, playing and talking to the students. In 1974 she played at the funeral of a man she admired deeply, Duke Ellington.

Kansas City honored her by naming a street, Mary Lou Williams Lane, after her, and she received honorary degrees from Fordham University, Manhattan College and Loyola University. Despite her enormous energy and prolific composing, Mary Lou Williams never became a "big" name. She was known and appreciated by devoted followers and fellow musicians and that's what she really seemed to care about. "She was more interested in growing than attaining fame," Father O'Brien explained. "She kept changing her style and was often overlooked in the jazz annals because she couldn't be pigeon-holed."

Never having signed a major recording contract was certain to have been a disadvantage. She recorded on lesser known labels and went unrecorded from 1941 to 1943. When offered a movie part, an opportunity other musicians would have eagerly accepted, she declined, saying she didn't like the idea of cameras on her. "Mary Lou was shy," Father O'Brien said. "She wasn't flashy, didn't use tricks, and never pursued publicity." Marian McPartland remembered Mary Lou as very quiet most of the time. "But then when she was relaxed, she'd giggle and laugh a lot," she said.

Perhaps the training she received from her husband John Williams during their time with the Kirk band had something to do with her modesty. Mary Lou had perfected an introduction that she was so fond of, she played it over and over. One day, he got fed up and knocked her off the piano stool. "You don't play the piano that way," he said. "Just because you did that 'Twinklin',' you think you're something."[27] Mary Lou kept his reprimand in mind whenever she felt her ego swelling from the praises of her listeners. Though her two marriages didn't last, she remained friends with her husbands and boyfriends. After a year or so, she'd back off from a relationship, perhaps to preserve her independence.

"I'm a loner," she'd say. "Music is my constant companion." But there were times when she gathered people around her, and she liked buying gifts for others, always taking time to shop while in a new city. "Mary Lou was a very good cook," Father O'Brien said. "She went to the market almost every day, and could make terrific Chinese food entirely from scratch." She also loved playing cards, something she had learned early as a way to fight boredom while on the road with a band. Skillful at hearts, poker and pinochle, she was always willing to play a few hands.

In 1977, Frank Tirro, chairman of Duke University's Music Department, invited her to come to Durham, North Carolina. After considering the offer, she decided it would be the perfect place to share the endangered music. She signed an artist-in-residency contract and moved south at the age of 67. Her Inaugural Concert took place in the Baldwin Auditorium on December 10, 1977. Her "History of Jazz" classes at Duke were so popular that 550 students were turned away one term. With Father O'Brien as her teaching assistant, the engaging dark woman exposed rock-age youngsters to the blues, the spirituals and jazz. Local sales of jazz albums increased dramatically within a short time after Mary Lou arrived. "You can't teach jazz from a book," she always said. During her classes she encouraged students to carefully listen to her play, then join in with their own vocal improvisations, to really "get into" the music. Only then could they realize the happiness and peace that jazz brings.

Mary Lou told them that jazz is an indigenous black American art form, not African inspired at all. Her good friends Erroll Garner and Art Blakey strongly shared the same opinion. "It was born out of the sufferings and joys of the black man," she said. "That's why it is so important that we don't lose it."

After Mary Lou's classes, stragglers often hung around with the hopes of talking to her. They were usually troubled by drugs, family tensions or identity problems. She drew them like a magnet. They felt they could trust her and were open to her suggestions on how to cope better with their difficulties. Under her gentle understanding always lay the belief that one must help oneself, and she encouraged them in that direction.

She composed for the Duke Wind Symphony and gave private lessons in her home. At first she missed New York City but came to love Durham, seldom returning to her apartment in Harlem. Mary Lou was still free for concert dates and recording sessions. *Jazz Women: A Feminist Perspective* was issued by Stash Records in 1977. The collection of 34 jazz performances of women musicians includes recordings from 1923 to 1957.

The liner notes for the wonderful collage were written by Mary Lou: "I never thought about anything but the music inside of me. I guess what happened to me was really unusual for a woman, as during that time a woman was supposed to stay home in the kitchen." Her notes reminisce about the early women of jazz and include the following comments:

"My entire concept was based on the few times I was around Lovie Austin. She was a greater talent than many men of this period."

"Lil Armstrong was another fantastic female of that time. Here she moves in good rhythmic patterns — no flaws, straight ahead, and again the playing is strong."

"Valaida Snow [vocalist and trumpet player] was so exceptional. She was hitting high C just like Louis Armstrong."

"Una Mae Carlyle was a very beautiful woman. She was one of Fats Waller's favorites–he was supposed to have trained her."

"Norma Teagarden has always been a fine pianist. Jack and Norma were wonderful."

"Dardanelle plays a good piano, too."

"Vi [Viola Burnside] really plays fine. That's good strong tenor."

" 'In a Mist' is one of my favorite things. Marian [McPartland] can sure play a ballad."

"Mary Osborne is really terrific — the most amazing woman I know on guitar."

"I saw Beryl Booker in Philadelphia last year. She plays some crazy beautiful harmonies."

"Sarah McLawler gives us some good soul music...excellent organist."

I'm glad Melba's here. She's a real musician and I love her." (Trombonist Melba Liston, scored and conducted the pulsating "Praise the Lord" and "Anima Christi" on the *Mary Lou Williams* album for Folkways Records.)

"Kathy Stobart is good, too. She has one of my favorite sounds on tenor."

"This *is* a nice collection," she concluded.

Mary Lou Williams — The Asch Recordings 1944-1947 came out around that time. It is a collection of 35 sides of Mary Lou playing solo, with small groups, with big bands and as part of a trio with Al Hall on bass and Bill Coleman on trumpet. These recordings give a captivating account of jazz during a highly creative period.

In 1978 she appeared at two very different events: "Mary Lou Williams and Cecil Taylor Embraced," a concert which teamed her with the avant-garde Taylor at Carnegie Hall, and a concert with Benny Goodman celebrating the 40th anniversary of his 1938 concert. That was also the year that President and Mrs. Carter invited prominent jazz musicians to the White House for a tribute to jazz. Mary Lou attended, was reunited with many old friends, and flashed her contagious smile for photographers while posing with first lady Rosalyn.

Her album, *History of Jazz*, also came out on Folkway Records in 1978. Moe Asch, who previously had released the Asch Recordings of Mary Lou's work during the bop years, had finally persuaded her to find time to do the history he suggested.

When it was discovered Mary Lou had cancer, she accepted it with the same patience and determination she applied to her music. "She handled her illness very well," said Father O'Brien. "Her music eased her pain."[28] The reserved performer never considered herself anything but a musician and in spite of surgery and follow-up treatments, she continued to work the last two years of her life. She even started her autobiography, *Zoning the History of Jazz*.

For an Atlanta concert in August 1980, Mary Lou was invited to perform with the Clark College Band. "All four of the black colleges in Atlanta are good," her step-brother Willis said, "But of course I was pleased that she was to play with my Alma Mater. She sent the music to the band so they could practice a month before the concert. Then she came a few days early to rehearse and give them insights into the music." Willis went on to say that the concert was a gala event. "Mary Lou performed with the band. They played 'The Land of Oo Bla Dee,' and 'Rosa Mae.'"

She played her last concert in Tallahassee in 1980 and was warmly received by the crowds. Mary Lou courageously returned to her music after each operation, and after radiation treatments in October 1980, she came out of the hospital to play a Mass at Sacred Heart Cathedral in Raleigh. Five Duke students sang the Mass. By Thanksgiving the treatments were taking a toll, and Mary Lou was unable to teach class much of the time. Marian McPartland said of her friend, "Mary Lou tried to play and do things for the kids right up to the end. We talked on the phone and she'd say, 'Well, I'm not at school, but I'm doing some arranging and the kids are bringing things to me.'"

In January, she was awarded a grant by the National Endowment of the Arts. A piano concerto which would reflect the history of jazz was under way. Interviewed that month by the *Greensboro Daily News*, she said of jazz, "It is God's music and will never die."

In February, Father O'Brien planned a Valentine Party at Mary Lou's house on Shepherd Street, inviting over sixty guests and arranging for Joanne Burke to film it. Mary Lou was surrounded by those who loved her. That was the last time she played the piano. She spent two days in March with Martha Oneppo, reminiscing the past seven decades of her life. After that she was in and out of the hospital, attending Duke symphony rehearsals under conductor Paul Bryan or planning the Mary Lou Williams Foundation.

"Because musical talent becomes evident early, like an aptness for math or science, Mary Lou wanted to focus her efforts on teaching jazz to promising children," Father O'Brien noted. "She felt that would insure the survival of the music." She decided to turn her entire estate over to a foundation which would serve a two-fold purpose: to grant scholarships and to provide one-to-one instruction for gifted children between the ages of six and twelve.

In early May, Duke University bestowed upon Mary Lou Williams its Trinity Award, praising her accomplishments as an artist and humanitarian. Part of the citation noted, "The latest decade of your life, a time usually reserved for retirement, has seen the full flowering of all your talents and gifts."

Mary Lou spent her last weeks at home, cared for by hospice workers and visited by her friends. She died on May 28, 1981. On June 1, a jazz funeral Mass was celebrated in honor of Mary Lou at St. Ignatius Loyola in New York City. Dizzy Gillespie, Marian McPartland and Rose Murphy were among those who performed her music in her honor. Excerpts from her three Masses were played and sung. "No woman instrumentalist has meant more to jazz than she," eulogized jazz writer Gary Giddens.

The following day, in the Church of Saints Peter and Paul in East Liberty, Pittsburgh, her burial Mass was celebrated. In lieu of flowers, mourners were encouraged to contribute to the Mary Lou Williams Foundation.

Later in June, the Universal Jazz Coalition in New York City paid tribute to Mary Lou Williams, who was on the board of directors. The memorial concert, under the direction of Cobi Narita, brought together the beloved pianist's friends in jazz.

Early in 1982, a four-part jazz series, "Swingin' the Blues," was shown on public television. One program was made up of musical segments of a concert she played in Lincoln, Nebraska, just months before her death and her own memories of her "jamming" years in Kansas City. The series was hosted by pianist Billy Taylor.

The works of the eminent artist are preserved on tapes and recordings. A documentary film covering concerts, degree awarding ceremonies and visits to Atlanta and Kansas City will be an inspiration to those following after her. Being female and Black didn't stop Mary Lou from embracing and cultivating her awesome talent.

A few months after her death, the Clark College Band of Atlanta traveled to a jazz festival in Denmark. They performed Mary Lou's music and were enthusiastically received. Her legacy seems secure.

[1]Duke Ellington, *Music Is My Mistress* (Garden City, N.Y: Doubleday, 1973).

[2]Mary Lou Williams, Liner notes on "Jazz Women: A Feminist Perspective," Vols. I and II, Stash Records, Inc., 1977.

[3]*Ibid.*

[4]Barbara Rowes, "From Duke Ellington to Duke University, Mary Lou Williams Tells the World: "Jazz Is Love," *People Weekly*, May 1980.

[5]Whitney Balliett, *Improvising, 16 Musicians and Their Art* (New York: Oxford University Press, 1977).

[6]Barbara Boughton, *Greensboro, N.C., Daily News*, Feb. 8, 1981.

[7]Whitney Balliett, *Improvising — 16 Musicians and Their Art.*

[8]*Ibid.*

[9]Nat Shapiro and Nat Hentoff, *Hear Me Talkin' to Ya* (New York: Rinehart and Co., Inc., 1955).

[10]Balliett, op. cit.

[11]Mary Lou Williams, Text of Recording of "The History of Jazz," FJ 2860, Foldway Records and Service Corp., New York, 1978.

[12]*Current Biography Yearbook 1966* (New York: H. W. Wilson, 1966).

[13]Balliett, *op. cit.*

[14]*Ibid.*

[15]Arnold Shaw, *The Street That Never Slept — New York's Fabled 52nd Street* New York: (Coward, McCann, & Geoghegan, 1971).

[16]Balliett, *op. cit.*

[17]Shaw, *op. cit.*

[18]Rowes, *op. cit.*

[19]Mary Lou Williams, Text of Recording of "The History of Jazz."

[20]Shapiro and Hentoff, *op. cit.*

[21]*Leanard Feather's Encyclopedia of Jazz* (New York: Bonanza, 1960).

[22]Shaw, *op. cit.*

[23]Mary Lou Williams, Text of Recording of "The History of Jazz."

[24]Balliett, *op. cit.*

[25]Debbie Fowler, "Married to Jazz," *Durham [N.C.] Herald Sun*, November 13, 1980.

[26]Rowes, *op. cit.*

[27]Balliett, *op. cit.*

[28]Teresa Damiano, *Durham [N.C.] Herald Sun*, May 29, 1981.

V

Women at the Keyboard

From the turn of the century women were involved in the new music, most of them as pianists. Billy and Lisetta Young, parents of tenor saxophonist Lester Young, traveled with a band, Lisetta playing the piano. An all-women's jazz band in Chicago featured Ethel Minor on piano. Lucy Williams was pianist for the Williams Ragtime Band, a Louisiana family touring throughout the state. In Washington, D.C., young pianist Gertie Wells became celebrated for her piano work with her own outstanding band.[1]

During the 1920's women ragtimers were in demand. Those working on a regular basis included Luella Anderson, winner of a ragtime contest in St. Louis, and Laura Brown of Newark. In Chicago, women made up the deficit for the short supply of orchestral pianists, though not one white woman became prominent in the field. One of the better known musicians was Lottie Hightower, wife of trumpet player Willie Hightower. Trained at Boston Conservatory, she led an 11-piece band, Lottie Hightower's Night-Hawks Singing Orchestra, which included musicians who had played with King Oliver's band. Willie later toured with his own group on the Pantages circuit from Los Angeles to Chicago. According to Earl Hines, while on the road Willie wrote numerous letters to Lottie and was his happiest when the mail would catch up, and he'd receive two or three letters from her.[2]

In 1921 a petite Creole musician named Bertha Gonsoulin was discovered in San Francisco by Baby Dodds. Bertha had already learned a lot from Jelly Roll Morton and despite her smallness, could play in a room-rocking style. She joined King Oliver's Creole Band as a replacement for Lil Hardin who was ill in Chicago and played with the band for about a year. She later returned to San Francisco to become a fine composer and musical instructor.

"Queen" Victoria Spivey, one of eight children, was born in Houston, Texas, around 1910. Musically precocious, she made her stage debut at 12, her record debut at 16, and was working at the Lincoln Theatre in New York City by the time she was 17. She sang, played piano, organ and ukelele and composed. "Black Snake Blues" was one of the earlier tunes she wrote. During the 1930's she led Lloyd Hunter's Serenaders and was featured with Jap Allen's Cotton Pickers. Victoria was recorded many times with top musicians such as Louis Armstrong and Henry Allen, and also appeared as a solo, in a duo, and as a touring artist in the late 1940's with Olsen and Johnson. After a hiatus in the 1950's, she resumed work in clubs, on radio and on television. The multi-faceted musician launched her own successful recording company in the late 1960's and continued to perform at blues festivals both at home and abroad.

Among the many women pianists in the Chicago area were Gladys Palmer; Garvinia Dickerson, who appeared with her popular Gold Coast Syncopators; Margie Lewis; Ida Mae Maples, who led the Melody Masters; pianist/bandleader Emma Smith; and Diamond Lil Hardaway, who at one time was with King Oliver.

Louisiana-born Nellie Lutcher joined the Clarence Hart Band when she was only 15. Her father was a bassist in the band that was paid less than two dollars a night. A few years later she headed for the West Coast where she was continually in demand for club dates. In 1939 she and her band played nightly aboard the *S.S. Texas,* a palatial pleasure ship anchored in Santa Monica Bay. Nellie introduced sizzling songs into her performances and was soon accompanying herself at recording sessions. She also composed tunes which became hits, among them "He's a Real Gone Guy" which was recorded by Ramsey Lewis in 1965 and reissued in its original form in 1978. After being away from the musical scene for several years, Nellie resurfaced in the early 1970's to perform at top New York music establishments.

Una Mae Carlisle began her successful career after being discovered by Fats Waller in Cincinnati in late 1932. She worked with him for a short time, then went out on her own. Eventually she toured Europe and enjoyed a long engagement in Paris. On recordings made by Una Mae Carlisle and Her Jam Band, Una Mae played the piano and did the vocals. A 1940 disc of "I Met You Then, I Know You Now" includes sidemen Benny Carter on trumpet, Slam Stewart on bass, Zutty Singleton on drums and Everett Barksdale on guitar.

Una Mae was also a composer whose tunes included "Walkin' By The River" and "I See A Million People." She did some radio and television work in the late 1940's, but because of illness retired in the mid-1950's. The talented woman, not yet forty years old, died in 1956.

Mary Lou Williams' contemporary and closest rival among

woman pianists in Kansas City was Countess Margaret Johnson who substituted for Mary Lou with the Clouds of Joy. She was a single attraction in clubs and jammed with the best musicians around, but recorded only once, backing Billie Holiday on four sides cut in 1938. Her self-assurance and polished technique are evident in her eight-bar solo on "You Can't Be Mine." She also worked with Harlan Leonard's band.[3]

Women pianists emerged all over the country. Drummer Gene Coy came out of Amarillo with his Happy Black Aces and played all over the country. His wife Ann was an excellent pianist with the band. Though the group was popular for over fifteen years, their music was never recorded. Kansas City pianist Edith Williams often played all night long for a dollar or two. Nancy Trance, too, played ragtime in Kansas City, but was never recorded. Charlotte Mansfield was another talent whose work eluded the recording studio. She was active in Kansas City as a single and a small band pianist who played the blues and vocalized in a gravelly voice. Pittsburgh had its own musical heroine Gertrude Long who led her Rambling Night Hawks. The band played for regular radio broadcasts and confronted other bands in musical duels which lasted until daybreak. Chicago's Grand Terrace was a mecca for jazz musicians. Jane Prater was one of the intermission pianists there around the same time as Gene Rodgers and Teddy Wilson. Christine Gassi also played around town. Touring bands throughout the Midwest featured Orvella Moore and Victoria Raymore. In New York City women pianists were plentiful. Frances Faye and Cleo Desmond were just two of the many crowd pleasers working at that time. Myrtle Jenkins, an accomplished blues player, provided pianistic support for blues singers such as Bumble Bee Slim.

In 1937 The International Sweethearts of Rhythm was formed. Some of their early performances raised funds for a black school in Mississippi. This finely-crafted ensemble, seated on a heart-decorated stage, was known for its Basie sound. The 16-woman band led by Anna Mae Winburn gained wide popularity and performed together longer than any other all-women's group. Johnnie Rice, coiffed in the popular upswept style of the day, was the orchestra's pianist. Jackie King replaced her in the 1940's and took part in the recording session of "Tuxedo Junction." Pianists with Ina Ray Hutton and Her Melodears (second only to the Sweethearts of Rhythm) included Gladys Mosier and Mirriam Greenfield, who can be heard on "Witch Doctor" and "Wild Party," recorded in 1934. Ohioan Rose Murphy began her long varied career in Cleveland where she played with a dance band while studying to become a teacher. Later on, concentrating more on the vocal aspects of the music, she became known as the "chee chee" girl. Her talents were in demand throughout the United States and Europe. Her swinging style was recorded, and she appeared in many important piano rooms and at top jazz festivals into the 1980's A 1940 recording of Joe Brown and His Band doing "Beaumont Street Blues" lists pianist Jewel Paige on piano and vocal. Marguerite Rosson was a graduate of Chicago Musical College who played at the Delphi Theatre in Chicago. Vivian Glasby worked in the Chicago area with Fletcher Henderson and His Orchestra. She and trumpet player Valaida Snow were recorded with the band in 1945. Sarah Vaughan and Earl "Fatha" Hines delighted listeners with their piano duets. Camille Howard was a first-rate blues and boogie player (Camille's Boogie, Miraculous Boogie, Extemporaneous Boogie), who led a trio in Washington, D.C., and was also a member of the Roy Milton band.

Dardanelle Breckinbridge, a young musician from the South, worked in New York City with her own trio. She sang and played the piano and vibraphone. Known professionally as Dardanelle, she successfully performed and made recordings through the years. Still active on the music scene in 1982, she appeared in the Music Room at the Horn of Plenty in New York City to good reviews.

After listening to the music of Basie, Tatum and Ellington and doing her internship as a pianist with her high-school dance band, Blossom Dearie was introduced to New York audiences. Four decades later, after performing and composing both at home and abroad, her playing and childlike singing still draws listeners. The early 1980's found her playing duets with Dave Frishberg at Michael's Pub in New York and also performing at the Women's Jazz Festival in Kansas City.

Ruby Young never had to travel far from her hometown of Pittsburgh to support herself as a pianist-organist. Her trios always had sufficient bookings at top drawer establishments. Beryl Booker first played piano with small combos before going out on her own. She collaborated with Mary Osborne and June Rotenberg in 1946 to record "Girls in Jazz" (Victor). During the 1950's, the Beryl Booker Trio was acclaimed by jazz critics as a formidable female instrumental group. The trio toured Europe, was in demand for recordings and enjoyed extensive engagements during its brief existence. In 1978 Stash Records reissued "Mamblues" with Beryl on piano, Norma Carson on trumpet, Bonnie Wetzel on bass, Elaine Leighton on drums, Mary Osborne on guitar and Terry Pollard on vibes ("Jazz Women/ A Feminist Retrospective," ST-109).

Alice Coltrane came from a musical family in Detroit and began working in a trio during the late 1950's. While in Europe, she met jazz

great John Coltrane, whom she later married. She eventually joined his
quartet and continued his music after his untimely death in 1967.
Shirley Scott gained musical fame as an organist working with The Eddie "Lockjaw" Davis Trio. The blues-rooted player went on to work
and record with jazz luminaries Coltrane, Basie, Mingus and Ellington.
Jazz writer Stanley Dance equated her musicianship at the organ to
that of Mary Lou Williams at the piano. Shirley's trio appeared on New
York television shows and toured during the 1970's. In 1982 she was
one of the sidepeople recording with Dexter Gordon on his first album
for the Elektra/Musician label.

Terry Pollard's long successful career began in the 1950's when
she played with small combos. Her name was added to the roster of
fine woman instrumentalists when she joined Terry Gibb's quartet. She
later earned a reputation as an excellent vibraphonist, but piano was
her first love. She appeared with many jazz greats through the years
and was still making limited appearances in the late 1970's.[4] Another
keyboard artist gaining attention in New York City was talented Sarah
McLawler who played both piano and organ. She first played with jazz
trios and was to become one of the finest organists in jazz. She recorded such tunes as "Red Light" which was reissued 25 years later on the
Stash label. In 1982 Sarah presided at an Easter concert in Central Park
and appeared at The Central Hotel in Abu Dhabi where she was held
over for a long period of time.

Though she later concentrated her talents on the bass, playing
with luminaries such as Mary Lou Williams, versatile Carline Ray
worked for some time as a keyboard artist. She played both organ and
piano with Edna Smith's trio. Another pianist, German-born Jutta
Hipp, performed at the Hickory House and other establishments. For a
while the pigtailed musician led a trio with Peter Ind on bass and Ed
Thigpen on drums.

The future looked bright for a very young pianist named Elaine
Geller working on the road with the Sweethearts of Rhythm. While
still in her early '20's she made recordings and worked with Miles Davis
and musicians of his calibre when they came to Los Angeles. She also
played regularly with saxophonist Ivy Black's combo. "She was the jaz-
ziest, funkiest, feelingest piano player I've ever met," Ivy remembered.
"She died one night, after working an after-hours job with me in
Hollywood. She went home, fed her baby and died. I know had she
lived, everyone would have heard of her."

Four more familiar women whose piano work and compositions
were recorded were Julia Lee, Cleo Brown, Irene Armstrong and Norma Teagarden.

Julia Lee

Julia Lee (born in 1902) was a phenomenal ragtime pianist from Kansas City who played up until the day she died in 1958. Her death saddened her many fans who were devoted to the Kansas City celebrity. Julia's father was a violinist. By the time the youngster was four, she was singing with his string trio. She studied piano and soon was appearing with a young musicians' band. In 1916 she turned professional, playing piano in a Waller's style and singing for private parties and social affairs around the city. George, Julia's brother, was six years older than she. He organized a band upon his return from the Army, where he had played saxophone and piano in the United States Army Band. Julia worked with George's band from around 1920 until the late 1930's. She also played with other groups and with such first-rate musicians as Ben Webster, Lester Young, Count Basie and Hot Lips Page. Long residencies at Milton's made the talented pianist-singer a favorite of Kansas Citians. Her successful engagement at the Three Deuces in Chicago was one of the few jobs she accepted outside Kansas City.

In the early 1940's Julia toured, doing solo work. She was backed by Kansas City musicians for her first recording date for Capitol in 1945. Though by that time she was over 40 years old, her keyboard and vocal style had remained the same. Her recordings were best sellers. A few years later, during Hollywood recording sessions, "Julia Lee and Her Boy Friends" included Vic Dickenson, Red Norvo, Benny Carter, Red Nichols, Dave Cavanaugh and Baby Lovett.

She was in California during the late 1940's doing club and theatre appearances. In 1949 she performed for President Truman in Washington, D.C. Then she returned to Kansas City where she often played at the High Ball Bar and the Cuban Room. She continued to perform there in her highly identifiable manner until her death at the age of 56.

Cleo Brown

Cleo Brown is a classically trained pianist who was born in 1907. As a child, she played piano at Baptist functions in Meridian, Mississippi. When her father, a Baptist minister, was assigned to

Chicago, Cleo provided music for his congregation there and continued to study. Her older brother Everett, also a pianist, was a friend
of Pinetop Smith. They both played boogie-woogie for dances. It
wasn't long before young Cleo was converted to the lively music and
excelled at performing it. "My momma was a short little woman called
Dutchie," the engaging musician recalled in 1982. "Both she and my dad
wanted me to give up playing boogie."

In 1923 Cleo was presented to the Jamaican Musical Circle of
Chicago. Against her parents' wishes, the independent girl joined a
touring band and later appeared around the Chicago area at popular
jazz nightclubs. She was signed with Tex Guinan in 1932 and began
playing and singing on her memorable Chicago radio shows. Her
powerful left hand and sensual voice made a lasting impression on
those who listened to her renditions of "The Stuff Is Here and It's
Mellow" and "You're a Heavenly Thing." She had a loyal following of
musicians from around the area. Weekly broadcasts of Cleo and the
big bands of Ellington, Basie and others were welcomed by those eager
to hear good jazz.

In 1935 she replaced Fats Waller on CBS radio in New York. "I
was playing at the Three Deuces in Chicago as a specialty act," she
said. "The big bands voted for me to take Fats Waller's place when he
left for Hollywood to make the movie "Hooray for Love." During the
late 1930's, Cleo continued to work in New York City, playing theatres
and clubs in addition to her radio shows. She also made a series of
records for Decca. Her interpretations of "Pinetop's Boogie-Woogie"
was among the tunes recorded. Six years later, Pinetop Smith was
killed in a barroom brawl. The percussionist's recordings affected the
musical development of future jazz artist Dave Brubeck and others
who heard them. "I listened to her records in England," Marian McPartland said in May of 1982. "She was one of the earliest influences on me."

Cleo suffered bad health during the 1940's and moved to
California. In San Francisco, something happened that changed her
life. "I had a visitation in 1949," she said, "and the Lord showed me his
plan for me. It took me two or three years to find what He showed me."
Cleo was booked in Las Vegas, Denver and Pueblo in the early 1950's.
During the Pueblo booking, she took up religious studies and began
her work in nursing. "In 1953 I was baptized, and I haven't looked
back," she declared. She received her nursing license in 1959 and com-
mitted herself to that profession until 1973. Her absence from the entertainment scene caused her to be listed as "deceased" in jazz biographies.

The talented musician is very much alive but has come full circle
in her musical preferences. From the mid-1970's until 1981, she per-

Cleo Brown. (Courtesy Frank Driggs Collection.)

formed weekly on Denver radio shows under the name of C. Patra Brown. "I just took the Cleo out," she explained. The boogie idiom was replaced by slower inspirational music, the beauty of her full chords and rich voice remaining intact. "I don't play boogie anymore," she said. "I'm so afraid I'll keep the boogie beat when I'm playing. It fits in with all the gospel music, but I don't play much gospel, mostly just anthems and hymns." In 1982 Brown was playing for services and accompanying the children's choir and evangelical singers at the Park Hill Seventh Day Adventist Church in Denver. During the previous ten years she had been employed as a senior companion, a babysitter and a missionary nurse. The handsome woman carries out her work with dignified fervor. "I write songs," she said, "but I don't push them. I just

use them if I get the invitation." She has great affection for her son
Matthew and his wife. He is a singing evangelist and colporteur. The
amiable pianist spoke proudly of her three older grandchildren, who
attend college, and the youngest, still in high school. They all are
musically talented, and though they have since studied with other
teachers, they received their first piano lessons from their grandmother. The family is known professionally as The Adventones. "I
started them out, all right," she said, "and I thank the Lord for letting
me see them grow up." In spite of failing eyesight and arthritic hands,
the contented musician still plays the piano every day. "I praise the
Lord that I can do what I do," she said. "I guess I'll always be the Lord's
'little old girl.'"

Irene Armstrong

Irene Armstrong was born in Marietta, Ohio, and learned to
play the piano before she started school. When she was 18 she moved
to Chicago, where she got a job playing piano at the Book Store.
Colleagues Lester Boone and Sid Catlett played alto sax and drums
respectively. Chicago's South Side was a magnet for the name
musicians during the 1930's — Earl Hines, the Dodds brothers, Louis
Armstrong and others. Irene soon was leading her own bands, usually
all-male and always with solid musicians. The tiny pianist's exuberant
performance at the keyboard highlighted every appearance. At one
point Irene hired Dolly Hutchinson to play trumpet. Dolly was the
daughter of Pearl Hutchinson, Ethel Waters' accompanist. The band
played at the Vogue, the Cottage and other clubs in Chicago. For a
while Irene and two other women were booked into clubs as a playing-
singing trio, appearing on the same bill with musicians such as Ethel
Waters.

Irene met Teddy Wilson shortly after his arrival from Toledo,
where he had played for radio shows with Art Tatum. Teddy was appearing around Chicago in a trio. After a brief courtship, Irene became
Mrs. Teddy Wilson, after which she assembled yet another band.
When Teddy had the opportunity to move to New York to work and
make recordings with Billie Holiday, Irene gave up her band work. The
Wilsons eventually separated and Irene began composing. Of the many
tunes she wrote, "Some Other Spring" (with lyrics by Arthur Herzog)
was readily accepted by both instrumentalists and vocalists. Art

Tatum, George Shearing, Charlie Byrd all recorded it, as well as Billie Holiday, Dakota Staton and Carmen McRae. Irene later married Elden Kitchings and in spite of an eye disease which grew progressively worse, continued to express herself at the piano, even after her sight was completely gone.

Norma Teagarden

"I think I am a better musician than ever," Norma Teagarden said recently. "I'm still learning though, and hope I always will." In 1981 the mayor of San Francisco proclaimed her 70th birthday "Norma Teagarden Day," after honoring her a few months earlier for outstanding public service, along with Turk Murphy and Earl Hines. The friendly pianist, noted for her stride piano style, celebrated her 70th birthday at the Washington Square Bar and Grill, playing her usual Wednesday night gig. "I have all the work I want, and that is a nice feeling," she said.

Norma can recall leaner days. On one occasion during the Depression, she was so broke while on the road, she had to hitch a ride home to Oklahoma in an open truck. The Teagarden house was a refuge for musician friends of Norma and her three famous brothers. Her mother and grandmother put them up and cooked for them between tours. Mary Lou Williams was one of the visitors and later recalled that Mrs. Teagarden sometimes sang opera for the guests. Norma worked with her brother Jack's big band for seven years during the 1940's and again later for three years with his smaller band.

Mrs. Teagarden taught Norma and her three sons, along with other paying students, to play classical music from piano instruction books. The musical family performed as a combo in 1918 with Mr. Teagarden on baritone, his wife on piano, 13-year-old Jack on trombone, 7-year-old Norma on violin, 5-year-old Charlie on trumpet and 3-year-old Clois on drums. Around that same time, Jack and his mother were a featured attraction at a local theatre playing piano-trombone duets. "I just drifted into it," Norma said of her life in music. "I started playing the piano when I was about six, although I played mostly violin all through my school years."

Her brother Jack was responsible for giving her a chance to work with a name band. She admits that being his sister helped her in the beginning. Her own competence at the keyboard quickly assured

Norma Teagarden. (Photo by Romaine.)

her of work with others including Wild Bill Davison, Ben Pollack, Matty Matlock and Pete Daily. "When I first started to play, it was difficult because I was a woman," she said. "The only women in the bands were singers. As I got more experience, it was easier." She always was paid union scale, but believed that jobs were harder to get because of her sex. She advises women jazz musicians to lead their own groups, as she did at different times over the years. "It's much easier if you are the boss," she said.

Norma almost always has worked with men and continues to "jam" with those who stop by while she is working at clubs. However, she did play with Ada Leonard's all-female group for nearly a year. The hotel-type band was mostly made up of competent women from Ina Ray Hutton's band of the 1930's. "I liked all of them," Norma said. "They were good readers, had excellent arrangements, and were well-rehearsed."

She feels that the music of the 1930's and 1940's was better than most of today's. Though she has tried to keep an open mind about it, she hasn't been impressed with much of the music over the past decade.

Of all the talented Teagardens, Norma is the only one still performing. Her father died when she was quite young, Jack and Clois are both gone, Charlie is retired and 92-year-old "Mama," who sometimes sat in with Norma on local jobs, died late in 1982. the last family appearance took place at the Monterey Jazz Festival in 1963 when Mama, Norma, Jack and Charlie performed together. Norma continues to play at jazz festivals in Monterey, Hollywood and Sacramento. Things have changed since she played concerts such as the Eddie Condon Town Hall Concert in 1944 with her brothers, but she keeps up with the times. During the past five years, she's performed in Europe, played on a cruise ship to Mexico and appeared at many jazz festivals and clubs around the San Francisco area. She enjoys sharing memories with her musician friends from over the years.

The veteran performer, while a guest on Marian McPartland's "Piano Jazz III" program for National Public Radio, reminisced in her deep drawl about earlier years. She also played several pieces including a lush version of "Stars Fell on Alabama" and an adroitly executed rag titled "Possum and Taters," which she learned from Mama. During the show, she joined Marian on impromptu versions of "Love Is Just Around the Corner" and "It's Almost Like Being in Love."

Norma has been married for 25 years to John Friedlander and lives in a memorabilia-filled apartment with a grand piano. John realized she enjoyed performing much more than teaching and so persuaded her to resume performing. "It would be terribly hard for me to give up playing," she recently admitted. "I hope I never have to." Looking back over more than a half century of playing jazz, Norma has concluded that a musician needs more than talent and technique. Being dependable and punctual, even on jobs she didn't like, was imperative. "You have to love the music more than anything else, and work hard at it," she said. "You also have to care enough about yourself to stay away from the drug and alcohol scene."

Many jobs for women pianists are in lounges where they perform solo. Norma feels those women need to learn hundreds of stand-ard tunes and must have the ability to play all types of music besides jazz, such as Latin, classical, pop. They should also be able to trans-pose well for singers they may accompany. "If you can sing, it makes it easier," she said. "I can't, and it has been a handicap."

The combination of marriage, motherhood and career as a pianist is not likely to be successful, according to her. She is convinced that marrying someone in the same business will work out only if the husband is as good or better than the wife. For a time, Norma was married to a musician. They worked together quite a bit so their hours were the same. Later on, she was single and able to tour and keep irregular hours with no entanglements. "If you aren't tied down by motherhood and running a home, I think you can make it," she said. "Have you noticed how many women musicians are single?" Despite occasional disappointments and frustrations (such as not feeling she played as well as she could have at times), Norma has an optimistic view of her life. "Music has been very good to me," she said. "I've never considered doing anything else."

[1]D. Antoinette Handy, *Black Women in American Bands & Orchestras* (Metuchen, N. J. & London: Scarecrow Press, 1981).

[2]Stanley Dance, *The World of Earl Hines* (New York: Scribner's, 1977).

[3]"Billie Holiday, The Golden Years," Columbia Records (C-3-L-40).

[4]Handy, *op. cit.*

VI

52nd Street

During the 1940's, "The Street" was a hectic center of musical activity. Between Fifth Avenue and Sixth Avenue, 52nd Street in New York was lined with clubs that featured jazz all night long. After the war, the nation's economy was good, and places like the Three Deuces, Onyx, Famous Door, Jimmy Ryan's and Kelly's Stable were jammed with customers. Musicians of different races and backgrounds came together for the first time to perform and exchange ideas. The use of microphones enabled small combos to produce large sounds. Improvisation reigned, and musical history was made. Besides Mary Lou Williams, other women pianists contributed to this epoch.

Marie Marcus

On May 25, 1982, Marie Marcus celebrated 50 years in the music business. A month later, her trio participated in the Kool Jazz Festival, New York's 10-day musical event. As musical director for the famous jazz club, the Columns in West Dennis, Massachusetts, the lively seasoned pianist is still very much a part of the music scene and never intends to quit. "If I couldn't play, I'd be dead in six months," she said.

Marie was born in Boston and raised in Roxbury in what is now called an extended family, with a grandmother, aunts and an uncle all under the same roof. She listened to Fats Waller and James P. Johnson on her mother's player piano and began taking lessons when she was eight. While still a teenager, she was hired to play on Bob Emery's radio program for children. When Bob Emery was called to New York to do a radio show, he asked Marie to go with him. She was 18 years old.

Marie Marcus.

Before long Marie was working as an intermission pianist in a bar. She and her friends frequently went to Tillie's Kitchen in Harlem. One night Fats Waller came in and played for the customers and then, after hearing Marie play, agreed to teach her when he had time. For two years he coached her, played duets with her and shared his ideas. He told her to strive for feeling, to come across to other people. "He was a great influence on me," she said. "His coaching meant a lot. I still strive for that feeling and to be a happy musician so my musical colleagues will feel the same way." Marie's inventive talents were soon in demand around New York. She played at speakeasies and eventually was hired at a spot on 52nd Street. "I was in New York at the time Hazel Scott and Mary Lou Williams were starting their careers," she said. "I was one of the very few white women around playing jazz then. Norma Teagarden, a fine Dixieland piano player, was another."

Marie started wintering in Florida with her husband Bill Marcus and their children. She joined Preacher Rollo's Dixieland group, which did regular radio shows, and enjoyed great popularity in the Miami Beach hotels. "I always worked with men," she said, "and never had a problem being accepted. I was lucky to receive encouragement from well-known musicians during the big band era. My biggest problem was the stupid statement, 'You play great for a woman.' " Marie worked with Bobby Hackett, Wild Bill Davison, and other name musicians in Boston, New Orleans and Cape Cod through the years. In 1963 she was enrolled in the New Orleans Jazz Museum by founder Dr. Edmund Souchon. Her television appearances included the Steve Allen, Arthur Godfrey and Dave Garroway shows. After being considered for the Lawrence Welk Show, Marie was deeply disappointed when she was turned down. JoAnn Castle got the job.

After 50 years in the business, Marie sees better times ahead for women musicians. The advent of more women's festivals is especially reassuring to her. Talent, technique and style are important, she admits, whether applied to performing the old or the new. But one thing above all Marie considers paramount. "For me, it's what comes from the heart."

Marian McPartland

If women jazz pianists have a godmother, it is surely Marian McPartland, who has become a symbol of achievement for women in music. She is a constant source of inspiration and encouragement to her sisters-in-jazz. Involved in dozens of jazz-related projects over the years, the pianist continually works for the advancement of the music and recognition of the women who perform it. Her presence is felt at jazz festivals around the world, (particularly ones that feature women), where she conducts workshops and talks with other women instrumentalists. Of prime importance to her is the time she spends in schools and on college campuses giving concerts and seminars. Her compositions have been recorded by prominent musicians and used for films. A familiar guest on the "Today Show," she has also hosted jazz series on both radio and television. Marian has also written for several publications and thoroughly researched a book on women's involvement in the music.

In addition to long annual engagements at the Hotel Carlyle in New York City, she began appearing with symphony orchestras in 1978 after deciding to include classical music in her repertoire. She seems to be many places at once and admits she wouldn't know what to do with more than two weeks off. "I had the work ethic instilled in me at an early age," she said. "My parents always had something for me to do. 'Don't lie around doing nothing,' they'd say."

Margaret Marian Turner was born in 1920 in Windsor, England, and began playing the piano at three, after hearing her mother play. She attended Stratford House for which she wrote the school song and designed the school emblem. She later studied classical music at the Guildhall School of Music in London, but by that time jazz had cast its spell. "I was influenced by everyone I listened to," she said. "I had some records of Cleo Brown's — boogie-woogie with rolling style. I listened to her, I listened to Mary Lou Williams, Duke Ellington and Hazel Scott swinging the classics. It's funny, because I never thought about women being different from men. There were a couple of women in England that I liked. Rae da Costa played on the BBC and another was Dorothy Carless who was in the four-piano group I first played with. She'd get up and sing a song, then sit back down and play with us again."

Marian's decision to tour with the vaudeville act didn't quite fit in with her parents' plans for her to enter a "respectable" profession like teaching or nursing. She played theatres all over England and in World War II joined ENSA (the English equivalent of USO Camp Shows), then transferred to the USO and was sent to France where she first had the opportunity to play with American musicians. In Belgium she met cornetist Jimmy McPartland of the U.S. Army Special Services. They formed a combo and entertained troops near the front. In 1945 they were married in Aachen, Germany, and played at their own wedding!

After the war, the couple returned to the United States and worked together playing Dixieland until 1950. By then Marian was aware of be-bop and ready to integrate the modern sounds with her traditional background. She opened in New York at the Embers Club with Eddie Safranski on bass and Don Lamond on drums. In 1952 a two-week engagement at the Hickory House was extended to last a

Marian McPartland. (Courtesy Betty Lee Hunt Associates.)

year, and Marian's reputation as a jazz artist was established. The Hickory House was home base for her trio for the next eight years. Drummer Joe Morello was with her for four years until he left to join Dave Brubeck. Her bassist was Bill Crow. The 52nd Street club was a stopping-off place for other working musicians who often sat in, among them Benny Goodman, Duke Ellington and Oscar Peterson. Marian's experience with the finest jazz artists and her facility to assimilate the best of what she heard helped her become a capable polished musician who never had a problem finding work despite being white, British and female.

Marian's forte has always been her inpressionistic ballads, which she seems to become part of. Her chordal brilliance, love of

melody and appreciation of good lyrics result in deeply felt interpretations which the audience can share. The pianist does not limit her
repertoire to standard ballads, however. Alec Wilder wrote several
tunes especially for Marian, who recorded an album of his music and
played his "Fantasy For Piano And Wind Ensemble" with the Duke
University Orchestra. She also confidently introduces the music of Ornette Coleman, John Coltrane or Chick Corea to her listeners with
whom she enjoys an easy rapport. "Although I'm not into playing
avant-garde music, I love to do some real free, way-out things just to
show I can," she said. "It's a lot of fun, but a little of it goes a long way.
I won't do that on a steady diet because I think I'd lose my audience if I
did."

The melodic qualities so evident in many of her compositions
have resulted in others writing lyrics to her tunes. Johnny Mercer
collaborated on "Twilight World," and Peggy Lee wrote lyrics to "Afterglow," changing the title to "In the Days of Our Love." "She said she
couldn't work with my title," Marian said, "but I didn't mind that she
changed it because she wrote such a beautiful lyric to it." She favors
provocative titles such as "Ambiance" and "Glimpse," the latter
revealing "...a little glimmer of sanity once in a while, a little fragment
of melody. It reminded me of someone peeking through the blinds. 'Afterglow' is self-explanatory, the feeling that hangs on after a love affair
is over. That actually came from a very real-life situation."

Though the McPartland's are divorced both musically and
matrimonially, they share halves of a townhouse in Long Island and often see each other. Jimmy praises Marian's playing abilities while she
credits "the old man" for introducing her to the New York jazz scene. It
was during the late 1950's that Marian's trio first ventured into a school
to play for children who had never been exposed to jazz. The response
was so gratifying that she set upon a crusade to bring her music to
those being fed only rock music by the media. "It's sold to us all," she
said. "Whoever controls the media controls what is played on the air.
It's like an unseen hand. Unless a kid is strong-minded, he goes along
with it to avoid being square. It seemed such a shame that some of the
kids hadn't heard the word 'jazz.' One day I asked a boy what it meant
and he replied, 'That's music for old people over 30.' " After successful
school concerts in Detroit, Chicago, Fort Lauderdale, Miami and
Columbus, Clem de Rosa (director of music at Walt Whitman High in
Huntington, Long Island) invited Marian to sit in with his band, a
frightening proposition for a mostly self-taught musician. That visit
paved the way for more assembly concerts during the 1960's through
the Performing Arts Curriculum Enrichment Program.

Soon Marian began wishing she could work with children in smaller groups, to achieve a more intense interaction. She began by visiting a typing class where the students typed along at a steady rhythm as she improvised a blues with a strong bass line. That led to English classes where she "played" adjectives for the students to identify, history classes where her trio put music to historical events and science classes where musical themes represented elements which were combined to form compound substances. Students and teachers alike were receptive to the spontaneous experiments. Next Marian decided to concentrate on younger listeners in kindergarten and early elementary grades. They were quick to identify a plodding elephant from her slow minor bass notes or a bird from her airy arpeggios in the higher register. Sometimes bongos, bells and other percussion instruments were handed out to enable the students to accompany their visitor's improvisations. "My favorite response came from a very young boy," Marian recalled. "He came up to me afterwards and said, 'Oh, I loved the music. I never knew a mother could play so good!'"

In 1974 Marian organized a nine-week pilot project in the Washington, D.C., Public Schools, sponsored by the National Endowment for the Arts. During that period she experienced a high point of her life. "I had been playing Duke Ellington's music for some high school kids and showing them improvisation," she remembered. "Duke's band was playing at Georgetown University so I asked him to come over. It was during the last year of his life and he was in a rather weakened condition. Another pianist played the warm-up, then I played a couple of numbers with his group before he came out. It seemed that even though he was sick, he got on stage and gave as much of himself as he ever had. He played for almost an hour. I don't think any of those kids will ever forget that he himself came and played for them."

It was while she was doing the musical experiments in schools that Marian discovered she saw keys in different colors. "I never thought about it," she said. "It just came out.... 'I see the color yellow when I play this chord.' I surprised myself when I said it. Working with kids brings out things you never knew. I see D as yellow and B as a dark-red plum color, and so on. I don't know where it came from. Every key has a different set of vibrations and I've always liked the sharp keys and more brilliant keys rather than F and C. They just seem more exciting to me, so maybe the colors go along with the feeling I get from playing them."

Over the years, Marian, along with Clark Terry and others, has been invited to judge college bands, many in state competitions. She

listens to different jazz bands and combos, comments on their appearance, choice of tunes, singles out good soloists and gives an over-
all critique of their performance. "Not so long ago, I judged six bands,"
she said, "and they were all very good. I couldn't believe the standard
of playing. Some of the kids were only 15 and 16."

Marian formed her own record company, Halcyon, in 1971, after dissatisfaction with major labels. "Interplay" was the first of many
albums released since then; the most recent one, "Live At The Carlyle"
(with Mike DiPasqua on drums and Steve LaSpina on bass), was
released in 1981. "Now's The Time" was recorded when Marian assembled a group of women musicians for a PBS program. That session included Mary Osborne on guitar, Dorothy Dodgion on drums, Lynn
Milano on bass, Vi Redd on alto sax and Marian on piano. She continues to record on other labels as well as her own. Though she feels
starting a record company is a complicated and time-consuming
project, she encourages other musicians considering it to go ahead.

In the late 1970's, Marian was invited to host a show for
National Public Radio featuring pianists who would discuss style and
technique and then join her at the piano. During the first series of
"Piano Jazz," her guests were Mary Lou Williams, Barbara Carroll,
Dave McKenna, Chick Corea, Bill Evans, Teddy Wilson, Bobby Short,
Ellis Larkins, Tommy Flanagan, Dick Hyman, John Lewis and Billy
Taylor. The second series, "Jazz Piano II," included Patti Bown, Hazel
Scott, Oscar Peterson, Hank Jones, Eubie Blake, Roy Kral, Cedar
Walton, Jay McShann, Duke Jordan, Roland Hanna, Ramsey Lewis
and Barry Harris. Marian feels she learned something special from
talking and playing with each of her guests. The series was rebroadcast
in 1982. Marian next hosted a television series for the Public Broadcasting Company titled "Women In Jazz," a highly informative
program about women's participation in the indigenous music throughout
the years. The pianist narrated the shows while seated at a piano,
playing from time to time to demonstrate a point about improvisation
or style. Film footage of the International Sweethearts of Rhythm and
other early women instrumentalists was reviewed, as well as films of
contemporary musicians at work such as Carla Bley rehearsing her all-
male band, and Joanne Brackeen producing her special fireworks at the
keyboard. "We did only one series of those shows," Marian said, "but
I'm hoping to do more."

Somewhere along the way, the energetic crusader decided to
take on another major project and write a book about women in jazz.
Research and interviews are time-consuming, but she fits them into her
busy schedule, between recording and symphony dates.

Marian made her symphony debut on April 1, 1978, playing Grieg with the Rochester Symphony. For a long time, she had been talking about studying again and felt the desire to perform with symphony orchestras. Besides the adventure of doing something new, she wanted to be in the position of having a classical piece in her repertoire when a concert date was discussed. She was encouraged to try the symphony circuit by her good friend and colleague George Shearing who had been playing Bach and Mozart on concert tours for some years. After choosing the Grieg Concerto in A minor, she took the music and an Arthur Rubenstein recording of it with her while traveling around the country playing jazz dates. When she later returned to New York, Ada Kopetz-Korf of the Manhattan School of Music tutored Marian and practiced with her until the Grieg piece was polished. The pianist's friend and teacher then played the orchestral part of the concerto when Marian tried it out on her listeners at the Cafe Carlyle prior to her debut in Rochester. Symphonies around the country have been featuring Marian McPartland as guest pianist ever since, requiring her to fly more than she cares to. "I certainly have a fear of flying," she admitted, "but I do it anyway. If it gets rough, I fly the plane right along with the pilot."

After the Grieg, she learned Gershwin's "Rhapsody in Blue," and though she once thought she didn't have the hands for Mozart, decided to try to master a concerto. Her own compositions "Ambiance" and "Willow Creek" have been arranged for the symphony and are usually on the program. She has admitted that she learned to appreciate the discipline required of classical musicians. "I've been practicing the 'Rhapsody In Blue' for a symphony date," she said. Every time I play it, I find new things I haven't discovered about the music. I'm also trying to write something for the symphony." There are no signs that Marian will ever drop out of the music scene nor does she want to. She would get itchy fingers if she took a few months off. "I just feel it's better to go on," she said. "Having work to do keeps one on an even keel."

The pianist is devoted to her friends. She recently dedicated an evening at the Cafe Carlyle to the esteemed late pianist Bill Evans, playing both his jazz waltzes and standards the two once played together. A few months earlier she had released on the Halcyon label a two-record set entitled "Marian Remembers Teddi" in memory of her good friend, singer Teddi King who died from lupus. Proceeds from the album went to the Lupus Foundation. Following the eulogy at Theolonius Monk's funeral, she played his "Round Midnight," as she had played compositions of other friends during previous funerals.

It's quite unbelievable that anyone as busy as Marian also finds time to correspond with friends, fans and students, but it's true. There are times people thank her for favors she doesn't even remember doing, it's become so natural to her. As for other women musicians, she doesn't feel she's put herself out that much or done anything she didn't enjoy doing. "If you're in a position to help someone, you should do it," she insisted. "You have a lot of chances to make that phone call, write a letter or do some little thing. My God, I had so many people help me, I'm just passing it on."

Some of Marian's letters were written to voice her opposition to the nuclear weapons proliferation, but she never received satisfactory answers, so decided to take part in the march on the United Nations in New York City in June of 1982. "Studs Terkel told me about it in Chicago," she said. "I said to count me in. If demonstrating will help any, I'll do it. The way things are going, there'll be no more world. It's insane!"

Marian's formula for leading an active life has produced favorable results. Her appearance belies her years, and her throaty laugh reflects her zest for living. She neither smokes nor drinks, and she stays in shape by walking a lot and gardening. "I've just edged the grass and replanted some things," she said. "I put out all the indoor plants. I like to putter around. I never get bored or have to go the the movies or watch television for something to do." The vibrant musician admits to loving good tea and makes it the proper way in a teapot with a teacozy. "Earl Gray's Breakfast Tea is good," she said. "I like it with milk and lots of honey. I've been reading up on honey. It's supposed to be terribly good for you in so many ways. I buy the real honey like gorgeous wildflower honey from Massachusetts. I don't like that commercial stuff. I've been thinking about keeping bees in the backyard. There are a lot of flowers in the area and quite a few bee people here on Long Island. I can't see myself putting on a bloody veil and gloves, so when it's time to get the honey, I'd bring in a professional beekeeper and hide in the house. The only reason I'm hesitating is that I have three cats that want to play with everything. I don't want them to get stung when the bees come pouring out of the hive and soar over the neighborhood into the various gardens. But a man I talked to said they won't stay in the backyard. They're much too busy going other places. 'So I'm thinking of getting some bees." For a woman with such a purposeful lifestyle, the addition of a hive of humming productive bees to her backyard seems quite fitting.

Hazel Scott

Despite the knowledge that she was terminally ill, Hazel Scott continued to perform her keyboard magic until a few weeks before her death in the fall of 1981. Every evening her trio played at Kippy's Pier 44 in the heart of the Theatre district, rocking the room with up-beat tunes or soothing listeners with poignant ballads. Jazz historian Leonard Feather later said, "I was most upset to hear of her death. In my opinion, she was a very underrated artist."[1]

Hazel Dorothy Scott was born in Port of Spain, Trinidad, and moved to the United States when she was three. Her father was a teacher and her mother an accomplished musician. By the age of five, Hazel was improvising at the piano. Too young to enter Juilliard School of Music at eight, she made such an impression on one of the teachers, Paul Wagner, that he agreed to teach her privately. Described as "Little Miss Hazel Scott, Child Wonder Pianist," she made her debut at a concert in Harlem when she was 13. The following year her father died, and her mother organized Alma Long Scott's American Creolians Orchestra. Hazel played piano and trumpet in the all-girl band. In 1938 she appeared in her first Broadway musical, "Singing Out the News," and she stopped the show when she belted out "Franklin D. Roosevelt Jones." A few years later, she delivered a stunning performance at the keyboard in "Priorities of 1942." *The New York Times* drama critic Brooks Atkinson lauded her performance: "She has the most incandescent personality of anyone in the show.... There is not a dull spot in her number."

Hazel also gained fame for her ingenious performances of her own modern jazz interpretations of classical works by Rachmaninoff and Liszt. Her debut at Carnegie Hall featured a syncopated arrangement of Liszt's "Hungarian Rhapsody No. 2." Her penchant for swinging the classics resulted in frequent radio performances. Because of the ASCAP (American Society of Composers, Authors and Publishers) union dispute with BMI (Broadcast Music, Inc.), standard tunes were not aired. They were replaced with fresh arrangements of classics familiar to radio listeners. Hazel's innovative jazz renditions of Bach and "In a Country Garden" were in demand. Shortly to follow was Hazel's departure for Hollywood, where she performed in "The Heat's On," "Broadway Rhythm," "Something to Shout About" and "Rhapsody in Blue," the film biography of George Gershwin. The pianist was popular in New York, from her first engagement at Tillie's Chicken Shack, to Kelly's Stable, the Hickory House, where she enjoyed a long engagement, and New York's Cafe Society Downtown and Uptown. She made her recording debut in 1939, the same year she appeared at the New York's World Fair.

In 1945 Hazel married Adam Clayton Powell Jr., the controversial minister and politician from Harlem. The marriage produced one son, and after a lengthy separation, ended in divorce. Always a champion of racial equality and liberal causes, Hazel donated her talents for various fund-raising events and was outspoken in her attacks against injustice. While still quite young, the entertainer's contract specified that she would not appear before a segregated audience. She stated, "What justification can anyone have who comes to hear me and then objects to sitting next to another Negro."

She lived for a while in Paris, then returned to the United States where she worked in Washington, D.C., and New York City. In 1978 she was received into the Black Filmmakers Hall of Fame for her cinema work. As long as she was physically able to perform in public, the gifted musician continued to offer her fans an extensive repertoire of compositions, all presented in unique Hazel Scott fashion.

Barbara Carroll

Barbara Carroll entered the jazz scene in New York in the late 1940's, when it wasn't considered "nice" to play jazz and when women musicians were seldom taken seriously. Nonetheless she landed a job at the Downbeat where Dizzy Gillespie was appearing. The attractive pianist with the light touch has been playing in all the important music rooms ever since.

Seven years of classical training and one year at the New England Conservatory of Music gave her command of the instrument, while her fervent interst in jazz never waned. The music of Nat Cole, Art Tatum, Teddy Wilson and other keyboard artists inspired her on her way to becoming a jazz pianist. "I did not consciously make a decision," she said. "It was inevitable." Early in her career, while working at the Embers in New York, she found herself playing opposite Art Tatum. "I was reluctant to play after he finished," she said, "but he was very kind and encouraged me to go on." Those first years were not problem-free, however. She can remember when women musicians looking for work were judged before ever being given a chance to play. "When I first came to New York, a friend attempted to

Barbara Carroll. (Courtesy Bert Block Management.)

book me on jobs by calling me 'Bobbie Carroll,' not mentioning my sex," she said. "When *I* showed up on the job, was the bandleader ever surprised!"

In 1953 Barbara appeared in a featured role on Broadway in "Me and Juliet," a Rodgers and Hammerstein musical. She played the part of Chris, the rehearsal piano player. The show ran from May 28, 1953, to April 3, 1954, totaling 358 performances. Barbara began recording in the 1950's for Discovery, Atlantic and RCA Victor. Discs were released on other labels through the years, the most recent ones being "From the Beginning" (United Artists) and her solo album, "Barbara Carroll, At the Piano" (Discovery). A reviewer in *People Weekly* praised her genius for "making every song a wondrous journey" and called the pianist a "pointillist and a watercolor heartbreaker."

She sometimes includes contemporary tunes in her repertoire, which is predominantly traditional. Flexible while performing, Barbara honors occasional requests during sets. She has not made the transition to electronic keyboards, preferring to present favorite standards and her original compositions in an intimate manner on an acoustic piano. Besides appearing at top clubs in New York, she has played in Chicago, Boston and London. She has toured Europe, Australia and Japan with Kris Kristofferson and Rita Coolidge and has participated in concerts with Benny Goodman at Carnegie Hall and Charlie Byrd at Disneyland. Guest spots on television include the "Today Show," "Tonight Show," "Merv Griffin Show" and the "Dinah Shore Show." She is a regular performer at jazz festivals and universities around the country. Her solo set at the 1982 Kansas City Women's Jazz Festival was a stunner, reminding critics of the harmonic piano work of Art Tatum. Previously, Barbara most often performed with a rhythm section of bass and drums. Her more recent solo engagements give her freedom to broaden her improvisational pianistic skills and to vocalize on romantic songs from the past. John S. Wilson, jazz critic of *The New York Times*, noted that, "Although her delivery is superficially cool ... her songs emerge with a vitalizing warmth." He also complimented her on "piano solos that one has come to expect of her — strong, two-handed, forcefully winning statements." Barbara thinks that continued experimentation will lead to growth in jazz. She most enjoys playing compositions with interesting harmonic structures. "They are the most fun on which to improvise," she said. "When I am playing my best, I feel as if I don't envy anybody in the whole world!"

After more than 25 years in the business, Barbara's is a familiar face on the Manhattan scene. The past few years she has played extended engagements at Bemelman's Bar in the Hotel Carlyle. When she begins playing in the dimly lit room, people listen. At home, where she lives with her husband and daughter, Barbara practices classical music to stay in top form, mostly Chopin, Mozart and Bach. To relax away from the keyboard, she dabbles in gardening and likes to read. For physical and mental fitness, she practices yoga and meditates. Barbara is a jazz veteran who works at perfecting and expanding her technical and improvisational talents, without compromising her feeling for a traditional genre of music. Her achievements surely make up for what she still considers the sharpest disappointment in her musical life. "I didn't win the title of 'class pianist' in my high school graduating class," she said.

[1]Correspondence with Leonard Feather, October 7, 1981.

VII

West Coast Musicians

The West Coast draws to its shores talented artists of every sort. Musicians are vital for the production of movies and television shows. And from Seattle to San Diego, the coastline is populated by jazz fans who attend festivals and frequent clubs where various styles of the music are played. It is natural that many women pianists make the area their home while they pursue the common goal of having a successful career as a jazz musician.

Betty Hall Jones

A Las Vegas columnist once described Betty Hall Jones as "a tiny 70-year-old black songstress-pianist who tore up the joint." Well-known in night clubs and hotels up and down the West Coast, the dynamic performer has such a devoted following that vacationers often plan their stay around her engagements. Barely five feet tall, with closely-cropped gray hair, Betty Hall Jones prefers to stand at the piano while performing.

Born in Topeka, she later moved to California. Betty studied piano from the age of five through her first year of college, then married and had two sons. In 1936, after she and her husband separated, she began her career in spite of her lack of confidence and in spite of family disapproval about "that type of music." But as she said of her decision, "I had two children to support."

Her first job was as a relief pianist-vocalist at the Reno Club in Kansas City, Missouri. There she met Count Basie who was just finishing an engagement. Betty then returned to California to play with Roy Milton's Band for five years in Los Angeles. When she struck out

Betty Hall Jones.

on her own as a single, it was in southern California, where she was raising her sons. In the 1950's, she extended her itinerary from Canada to the Southwest.

Betty recalled early incidents of discrimination. "I can remember when men would leave, one by one, when a woman was 'sitting in' " she said. "They claimed we couldn't keep time." "My favorite pianists were Mary Lou Williams, Art Tatum, Teddy Wilson, Fats Waller, Meade Lux Lewis, Pete Johnson, and Duke Ellington," she said. "I believe you should listen to everybody and take the best for yourself to help refine your gift."

Betty Hall Jones, besides being a fine player of Kansas City boogie, jazz and blues, expanded her performance to include calypso and show tunes and popular comedy bits which earned her the title "Miss Versatility." She gets involved with her fans, even taking down their addresses so she can keep in touch. And her audiences love her. "I have a person-to-person act," she said. "People say my music makes me and them feel better."

Betty has had her own duo and trio and in 1978 was co-leader of a women's Dixieland group called the "Satin Dolls." With Kay Blanchard on sax, Bonnie Janofsky on drums, Vi Wilson on bass, Eunice Dureau on trombone and Lynn Delmenco on trumpet, the band appeared at the Dixieland Jazz Jubilee in Sacramento. "I really enjoyed playing with that band," she said.

Betty Hall Jones plays benefits and visits nursing homes where many of the patients are younger than she is. "It makes me feel good to make them happy," she said, "and I realize how lucky I am."

During World War II, her performances with USO Shows were always well received. Her incredible timing and contagious humor made her a female counterpart of Victor Borge. Betty could sing, dance, ad-lib and make frequent costume changes without ever leaving her piano. One of the most memorable moments of her life came during one of those tours. "I was visiting a hospital ward, trying to cheer up the patients," she remembered. "I broke the silence of a battle-fatigued woman soldier. She smiled for the first time at a bit I did."

Betty's only regrets are that she wasn't able to break into the recording field and that women musicians, especially black ones, aren't given more opportunities to appear on TV shows. Without a schedule or an agent, she travels up and down the West Coast, delighting audiences in Seattle, Salem, Las Vegas, San Diego and Las Cruces, New Mexico. "I'm the Galloping Grandma," she said. "If someone wants me, they give me a call." Betty has become accustomed to being praised for her stamina and positive outlook. She is also getting used to standing ovations, like the one given her by 600 people after her one performance at a 1981 Bob Hope Charity Golf Tournament. Many times the seemingly tireless performer has thought of writing about her nearly forty years behind the keyboard. She also would like to share her love of life and music with the younger generation by giving programs in schools. "I've had some wonderful experiences," she said. "I just wish I were twenty years younger."

Joanne Grauer

Her exquisitely-sculptured face framed by long, tousled blond hair could grace a magazine cover, and her slender figure could easily belong to a fashion model. But more often than not, Joanne Grauer, a pianist of imposing skill and unequaled sensitivity, stays out of the limelight, preferring to teach, compose and do studio work.

She coached Barbara Streisand for the piano sequences in "A

Joanne Grauer.

Star Is Born," played all the piano solos for Academy Award winner Ellen Burstyn in "Alice Doesn't Live Here Anymore," and played on the sound tracks of "Lady Sings the Blues" and "40 Carats."

"I am a private person," she said. "My emotional structure and natural desire for home and security and sensitivity makes it difficult to be aggressive in the business areas and politics of music." When she does perform in public, it is usually in the Los Angeles area, and always to rave reviews. Whether executing one of her own original compositions or someone else's, Joanne dazzles audiences with her introspective interpretation, making every selection she plays uniquely her own. Often a few moments of silence follow the final note of a piece as her listeners emerge from their trance before they begin to applaud. "I was destined to be an improvisor," she said. "It was natural to me."

Though her parents felt a career in jazz was a terrible life for anyone, especially a woman, her teachers were very supportive. "The freedom that is necessary to any artist was quite threatening to my parents," she said. "They also thought it was a good way to starve, and in that they were partly correct. Making a living in jazz is nearly impossible, but because of my versatility, I've always made a good living from music, though not always jazz."

Joanne has studied classical music since the age of five and feels it makes technique possible. "All music is one," she said. "Bach aids in jazz ideas, Chopin in touch, and Beethoven in personal strength." Her father, a pianist who played at Ciro's and other clubs, first taught her to play. She then studied with other teachers before making her debut with the Million Dollar Theatre pit band. "My jazz teacher Sam Saxe was a major influence in my becoming a jazz pianist," she remembered. "My own favorites are Bill Evans, Horace Silver, Mike Garson, Chick Corea, Carla Bley and Keith Jarrett. They inspire me mostly and force me to reach."

Joanne began appearing at Donte's in Universal City in the late 1960's and often has been billed there through the years with Louis Bellson, Gabor Szabo, Bud Shank and others. Her trio, with Bob Magnusson on bass and Al Cecchi on drums, has also delighted audiences in numerous other area clubs. As Andy Williams' personal accompanist, she was on the road with him for six years and appeared on his televised Christmas specials. She also played for Paul Williams, Diahann Carroll, Pat Boone, Connie Stevens, David Cassidy, the Osmonds and other name singers.

Her concerts include the "Women in Jazz Series," at UCLA in 1978 and 1979, Los Angeles Pianists' Club Concert in 1976 and 1980 and a "Four Piano Concert" at Cerritos College, where she shared the stage with Pete Jolly, Paul Smith and Father Tom Vaughn. The audience was so thrilled that encores ran into seating time for the next performance. Joanne has also played in jazz ensembles with Terry Gibbs, Zoot Sims, Quincy Jones and Paul Horn. Her TV performances include "The Midnight Special," "The Jazz Show," "Today Show," and special interviews on ABC-TV News and other shows. Live theatre productions include "Hair," "Oh! Calcutta," "Tommy," "The Wiz" (in which she played all keyboards), "A Chorus Line" and "Appearing Nightly," Lily Tomlin's one-woman show in Los Angeles and San Francisco. Much of Joanne's time has been spent teaching at Dick Grove's music school in Studio City since 1976. She also teaches private students in her home.

"The highest moment in my career came when I was asked to record my first album for MPS Records," she said. "I felt happy, afraid, and all of a sudden, as if I had a terrific responsibility to be the best. It was very painful."

That first album, titled *Joanne Grauer, Introducing Lorraine Feather*, was released in 1978 and named by *Billboard* as one of the "Top Album Picks." Other albums followed, as well as featured keyboard work on discs by Stanley Turrentine, Andy Williams and others.

In 1980, Joanne Grauer was awarded a grant by the National Endowment for the Arts to further her composing and performing career. That was the third consecutive year she received the honor. Her fine compositional skills are evident in the more than 100 original pieces she has written, many of them musical portraits of people and animals. Joanne grew up loving animals and wanting to be a vet, so it seemed natural to combine her lifelong rapport with animals and her musical talents to compose animal portraits. Her first portrait was "Misty Dreams" which she composed as her German Shepherd, Misty, slept under the piano. She soon found (she's not sure how) that she could translate other animals' vibrations and feelings into melodies. Through her appearances on TV interview shows, Joanne has been assigned to compose over 100 original pet portraits. After spending some time with an animal, Joanne sets to music the individual mischievous, affectionate characteristics of a pet's personality. The piano composition is then transferred to a cassette tape which is presented to the pet's master. Some impressed pet-owners have requested portraits that depict their own personalities. While visiting the Los Angeles zoo, Joanne felt such compassion for a giraffe, she went home and composed a moody portrait, "Lonely Giraffe," a haunting, impressionistic piece which truly does make one perceive the animal's aching loneliness. Joanne has often considered working as an animal healer. She also thinks being a counselor in metaphysical psychology would be a worthwhile profession. "If I could no longer play, I would immediately begin to work on one of many ways to express my talents," she said. "As long as we're alive, there is so much to do and contribute."

Twice married, both times to musicians, Joanne feels that sustaining a successful marriage and career is a complex and almost impossible endeavor. Achieving a balance between her solitude and musical professional demands is a constant concern. "Knowing who you are and what you want are important," she said. "You must be willing to give up everything for music, for it is truly a 24-hour job, to master every human emotion and apply that to your instrument." West Coast critics attest that the subtle nuances of Joanne's lyrical artistry are increasingly reflected in her facial expressions as she gets lost in he music, her fingers caressing the keyboard. "I strive for perfection, complete communication, expression and honesty," she said. "Some people stereotype women musicians, but when they hear me play, they take me seriously. Most women jazz players lack drive and strength, but there do seem to be more good players now than when I was a teenager. I prefer playing with men and women who do not consider what sex they are, but are 'Instruments' of their art." Among the many supportive and helpful musicians in her life, Joanne mentioned Dick Grove, Michel LeGrande, Buddy Collette, Marian McPartland, Benny Powell and Louie Bellson. Roger Williams said she's very special, and jazz writer Leonard Feather is one of her solid supporters.

Joanne's studio work consists mostly of commercials, but she recently appeared in a pilot for a possible TV series. One project away from home was leading the Women All Stars at the fifth annual Women's Jazz Festival in Kansas City in March 1982. Her surging yet graceful piano work enchanted critics and audience alike. Listeners were keenly aware of the phenomenal creative forces the All Stars integrated into their closing night performance.

Whether at home or away, Joanne Grauer doesn't waver in her commitment to music. "I consider talent a great gift and responsibility, for music is the highest form of art. The universe itself is set up on a sound or tone scale. The rhythm of the planets and all of nature is music. This makes us very aware of our relationship to the earth, its animals, and to God. I strive to honor my place in this universe."

Barbara Sutton Curtis

In 1950, teenager Barbara Curtis spent every Sunday evening aboard a barge moored at the foot of Poplar Street on the St. Louis riverfront. She was pianist for the Dixieland Six which marched up the gangplank every week to the beat of "High Society" or "When The Saints Go Marchin' In." Jazz fans arriving for a three-hour concert followed the band to the barge's middle-deck ballroom for an evening of "hot jazz on the river." The combination of Dixieland jazz and the Mississippi was reminiscent of earlier years when the new music made its way north from New Orleans via excursion boats. Dozens of jazz greats perfected their musicianship while performing on the Mississippi. The Dixieland Six was led by Singleton Palmer, a bass horn and fiddle player who formerly had played with Count Basie. Al Gulchard, a native of New Orleans, played clarinet and Norman Murphy, who once played with Gene Krupa's band, blew trumpet. Sid Dawson of the St. Louis Stompers played trombone, and Elijah Shaw, a former minstrel and riverboat musician, presided at the drums. "The band accepted me with affection," Barbara said. "As I look back, I realize they treated me as an equal, even though they all had years of experience and I was just starting."

Barbara began playing when she was eight and studied classical music for fourteen years. She was greatly encouraged by her brother, professional pianist Ralph Sutton, a familiar name in jazz annals. The decision to become a jazz pianist was made in her teens, and she never regretted it. "I've had some of the happiest moments of my life playing jazz," Barbara said, though she admitted there were drawbacks. "I found I was vulnerable because of the late hours and not-so-safe neighborhoods. Another problem was sustaining the stamina to go on while keeping the other areas of my life in balance." Over the years, Barbara has entertained in New York, Tucson, San Francisco and Denver. She began her annual Ukiah community "classical jazz" concerts in 1977. Opening with her own arrangement of Fats Waller's "Ain't Misbehavin'," which has become her theme, she proceeded every year to entrall her audience of all ages from toddlers to senior citizens.

Before beginning each number, Barbara gave the audience a little background information about the composer's contribution to jazz and style of playing. Her physical strength was evident during her playing of demanding ragtime pieces and stride compositions by James P. Johnson, whom she admires for his effortless swinging style. She moved her audience with sensitively interpreted themes by Duke Ellington. Her selections included arrangements of Gershwin and Bernstein tunes, as well as rollicking Jelly Roll Morton numbers and "Finger Buster" by Willie "The Lion" Smith, which brought a standing ovation. One reviewer declared Barbara "a musical treasure" of the community.

Solo performances tend to make Barbara nervous, though she experienced the highest moment of her career while appearing alone. "I was giving a solo performance at the Inverness Music Festival in 1977, sharing the program with Norma Teagarden," she said. "I was playing for the people who would be critical of me and I was understandably nervous that I would play badly. About a quarter of the way into it, I relaxed and the joy I felt from letting people hear me as I had heard myself was wonderful." On another occasion her brother persuaded her to take over for him for a solo piano engagment in Denver while he was on a European tour. She again performed admirably and received very good reviews. "I was nervous," she said, "but Ralph knew I could handle it and told me so." Upon Ralph's return, he and Barbara pleased Denver audiences with their memorable duets at the club BBC. "My one disappointment is not having the opportunity to make a two-piano record with my brother," she said. "We are a lot alike in our styles, our sense of timing is like one heartbeat. Yet, we *are* different in our expression. I wish we could have passed this on."

Barbara strives to make every concert better than the last by improving her technique which she said often opens the gate to expression. She also is very aware of a sense of balance in her improvisation. She admires Oscar Peterson's technique and the good taste and balance of Marian McPartland. Other favorites include Dave McKenna, Bill Evans, Art Tatum and Fats Waller.

Barbara Sutton Curtis continues to perform at concerts and leads a quartet in which her husband plays drums. She never intends to stop playing. Just the thought brings her close to tears. "I would feel that part of me had died that I could never replace," she said. 'A career as a jazz pianist is difficult for a woman, who may have to choose between success and having a family, she feels. But she envisions a brighter future for women musicians. "I am delighted to see how the Women's Jazz Festival in Kansas City has taken off," she said. "The very fact that it is continuing, and successful, and bringing women musicians together, makes me feel that the future will be a better one."

Patricia Sea

Patricia Sea of Portland, Oregon, was hired for band work at the age of fourteen by the late Ron Leonnig and has been playing ever since around the Portland area. Her 25 years as a jazz keyboardist, either performing solo or with her trio, have been spent in clubs and at fraternal organizations and private parties. However, she became discouraged with trying to support herself by playing jazz so now she limits her performing to weekends. For the past several years, she has worked as a full-time government employee. "Inherit money," she tells other women who are thinking about embarking on a jazz career.

Patricia began playing the piano at five, and her mother encouraged her to continue. Her classical training gave her basic discipline and taught her phrasing and how to color and accent the music. During her high school years, she felt almost ostracized because she was so deeply involved with her music she had time for little else. Though she had to compromise along the way by expanding her repertoire to include other types of music, she always received equal pay and acceptance from other musicians, most of whom were men. The compliments that meant the most to her came one night in Paris. "I sat in with a band at the Blue Train," she recalled, "and after we finished playing, all the musicians told me I was really good." The pianist has never worked with other women musicians. "The ones I was interested in playing with seemed to feel threatened even by a sit-in with their groups," she commented.

Patricia's goal while performing is to sincerely present what she feels and to entertain the audience, regardless of the situation. Her favorite pianists are the late Vince Guaraldi (for his unique style), Roger Williams (for his liquid classics), and Marian McPartland (for her dash and verve). Patricia sometimes experiences a sence of déjà vu when starting the first set in a new club, but finds that playing one or two of her old favorites brings her out of it. "My only problem is transporting my equipment," she said. "I usually have to provide my own keyboards wherever I work."

She thinks the future for women in jazz will be better because they are interested more and more in becoming good, solid, dependable musicians and are willing to spend the long hours necessary to achieve their aim. "I would like to tell other women to take a chance, hang in there, but pack a parachute," she concluded.

Joyce Collins

When Dave Brubeck heard Joyce Collins play in the early 1950's at a junior college in Nevada, he advised her to move to San Francisco to study with his piano teacher. That's what she did. Then while earning her B.A. in music at San Francisco State, she received encouragement and support from the student director of the college jazz band, whom she later married. "Some people will do anything to get a good grade," the attractive brunette joked.

Joyce has never wavered in pursuing a career as a jazz pianist since she made the decision at the age of ten. "I wouldn't listen to *any* discouraging influences," she said. "My goal was always clear." Her first influence was Teddy Wilson, followed by Fats Waller and James P. Johnson. Four years of classical training advanced her technically, but she feels it can be a hindrance if one gets too tied to the printed page. Leonard Feather described her "tasteful musicianship" during a West Coast engagement as "technically adept but never flashy."

She has worked in jazz clubs in Las Vegas, Los Angeles, Mexico

Joyce Collins.

City, Paris and New York where Rex Reed called the trio (Bill Henderson, Dave Mackay and Joyce) "superb musicians" and "total pros, giving and sharing without egos." In the spring of 1982, Michael's Pub in New York City was the setting for "A Fusion of Ellington and Gershwin," which drew favorable comments from the critics. The program featured the trio's fresh renditions both of familiar tunes and of great but rarely heard Ellington ballads. The pianist's concert tours include those with Paul Horn and Bill Cosby. Among her albums are two made with Bill Henderson, "Live and the Times" and "Street of Dreams." The latter was nominated for a Grammy Award in 1980. "Moment to Moment" by the Joyce Collins Quartet was released in 1981 and was one of the five Top Album Picks by *Billboard*. Joyce was the first woman elected to serve on the Musician Union's Board of Directors and the first woman to conduct a show band in Las Vegas (as musical director for "Unusual We").

For ten years she was associated with Mary Tyler Moore Enterprises in a most pleasant occupation. She fronted the quartet that played during the warmup before the live filming of the "Mary Tyler Moore Show" and the "Bob Newhart Show." The musicians were free to play anything they wished during the three evenings every week at the TV studio. Joyce also made occasional brief appearances on segments of those two shows and those of two other MTM productions, "Rhoda" and "Happy Days."

Her income is supplemented by teaching. "It's very exciting to teach and see people develop musically," she said. "It's also very exciting to practice and see myself develop musically." Favoring both experimentation and tradition in jazz, Joyce said, "It has to move ahead but that doesn't mean it automatically gets better!"

Jimmy Rowles has been a favorite of hers for twenty years, and she credits him with sharing his harmonic ideas with her. "I probably listen to his records more than anyone's," she said. "He's so original, with great warmth and *all* music, no cliche's or showing off." She was also encouraged by Marian McPartland and Jeri Southern who coached her singing for her album, "Moment to Moment." Joyce remembered her first recording experience in 1961, when she made a demo record with Ray Brown on bass and Frank Butler on drums. "I sent it to Orrin Keepnews who was with the Riverside/Jassland label and signed it 'J. Collins,' " she said. "When I later went to New York, he was absolutely shocked and speechless. He was sure I was male and black. He put out my album and that was a *very* exciting event. I felt like Cinderella."

Joyce feels that the women's rights issue has raised the general consciousness level. Though she always received equal pay and refused to let discrimination stop her, at first she had a problem being taken seriously. "Many times I was not given a chance because of prejudice," she said. "Worse than that, agents I auditioned for told me I had no 'sex appeal.' What has *that* to do with music?"

A sense of humor and adaptability have seen her through some frustrating situations. She's often had to work in other areas of music in order to keep going. One of her ideas resulted in the publication of a jazz/rock piano book for children, which includes a rhythm section record to accompany the student. Joyce thinks jazz will always appeal to a small, but select audience, and had one word to describe the future of determined women jazz musicians: "Excellent!"

June Derry

"I can't even play chopsticks," June said. "I wasn't allowed to touch the piano until I started taking lessons when I was 12. From my classical training, I learned to read music and appreciate the value of scales and exercises." That classical training actually consisted of a total of 36 half-hour lessons from a country teacher. She learned to play jazz by listening to the radio, records and pianists that she admired and from that, she became a most capable musician. "When I heard the Paul Whiteman orchestra and Mary Lou Williams with Andy Kirk's band, I knew I wanted to be a pianist," she said.

Over the years, she has admired Bing Crosby's accompanist Buddy Cole, Norma Teagarden, Dixieland pianist Stan Wrightsman, Teddy Wilson, Bob Zurke, Mary Lou Williams, Barbara Carroll and Peter Nero. "My tastes are definitely not 'far out,' " she said. "I appreciate those who play with taste and are not too discordant." June feels much of the music now lacks the finesse of some of the older tunes which were executed by big bands with full sound and top musicians. Since the demise of big bands, she has concentrated on working solo in restaurants and on cruise ships. But at one time, she worked with many well-known performers at the Hangover Club in Hollywood, and she especially enjoyed being featured by Ben Pollack in several of his small groups with musicians Mel Torme, Barney Kessel, Phil Stevens and Morrie Stein.

She never experienced serious problems in being a woman musician, but does feel she was better accepted before all the "to-do" about ERA. She considers many other women musicians far superior to some of the men she worked with in bands. "I've heard quite a few so-called 'good men players' who were actually mediocre," she said. Some women, she thinks, lack the physical strength for big band and combo work, or *did* before the wide use of microphones. To her, the ability to adapt according to the requirements of a job and a proficiency in reading music are "musts" for consistently performing on a high level.

Working as a single, June concentrates on providing a good modulated type of listening music and a steady danceable beat. Her renditions of scores from Broadway shows by Gershwin, Rodgers, Berlin, and Porter are popular with her audiences. She also does stints with small jazz groups.

June has held jobs in other lines of work, but always returns to her music. At this stage in her life, she is interested in composing and is active in the other arts as well. Her piano work over the past few years for the cruise lines (Sitmar-Countess and the famous Pacific Princess of "Love Boat" fame) was done under her married name June Weston. "Although I have never made a great deal of money, music *has* enabled me to travel a good part of the world as a pianist," she said. "If I couldn't play, I'd miss it terribly."

Dorothy Donegan

"Flamboyant." "Outrageous." However critics describe her, Dorothy Donegan is a jazz legend whose technical brilliance impresses even those who don't approve of her vaudevillian antics. Almost 60, the volatile pianist still assaults the keyboard every time she's on stage.

Born in 1924 on Chicago's South Side, Dorothy began learning the classics while very young. She still dreams of a career as a concert pianist and continues her classical studies. While in her teens, she got sidetracked into playing jazz, and gave her first half-classical, half-jazz concert in Orchestra Hall in Chicago. The power and precision of the young pianist earned her good reviews and an invitation to play for Art Tatum, who was so awed, he agreed to tutor her. It wasn't long before the young virtuoso was invited to Hollywood to appear in the movie *Sensations of 1945*, with Eleanor Powell and W.C. Fields. After making her Broadway debut in "Star Time," she returned to the piano. Companies such as Decca, Victor and Capitol were just a few that recorded her work.

In 1952 she opened her own jazz club in Los Angeles. Dorothy divided her time between there and The Embers in New York where she broke house records and signed an unprecedented contract for sixteen weeks a year for ten years. Because of her wild behavior on stage, the Internal Revenue considered taxing the club for a cabaret act rather than for instrumental entertainment. A regular at the London House in her hometown Chicago and Jimmy Weston's in New York City, she had her audiences coming back for more. "Donegan Walk" with its relentless walking left hand and "Old Black Magic" with its stabbing chords and contagious rhythm defied listeners to sit still. Her penchant for crossing freely between the classics and jazz brought chiding remarks from critics who nevertheless had to admire her formidable virtuosity. It was also during the 1950's that she studied sociology at the University of Southern California and gave birth to the first of two sons. She retired for a while in the mid-'60s, but then resumed club and concert work.

The entertainer was received enthusiastically on the European concert circuit, and in spite of having to demand equal pay for her appearances, felt more valued as a professional artist than she did at home. However, when she later played during a tribute to Josephine Baker in New York City, the audience gave her a standing ovation. In 1976 Dorothy was featured with the New Orleans Philharmonic at Tulane University, where The Jazz Archive is located. She played Grieg's Piano Concerto with no embellishments or improvisation. Two years later, the mayor of Chicago declared her birthday "Dorothy Donegan Day in Chicago."

Through the years, the fiesty pianist has not been one to mince words. She is an outspoken feminist who is vigilant against sexist prejudice. After three marriages, Dorothy told Pop/Jazz writer Stephen Holden of *The New York Times*[1] (October 9, 1981, p.22), "I think the pattern is trying to tell me something. I don't think an entertainer should be married, because you have to practice eight hours a day, and nobody can stand that kind of competition." That year Dorothy appeared at Michael's Pub in New York City for a month's engagement and gave a rousing performance at the Kool Jazz Festival in New York City. Among her 1982 dates were returning to the Kool event; performing with her trio at the Center for the Arts at the State University in Purchase, New York, and at the Minneapolis/St. Paul Kool edition; and performing at the Berne Jazz Festival in Switzerland with Dizzy Gillespie, Ella Fitzgerald and Betty Carter. Yet another record, "The Explosive Dorothy Donegan," was released in 1982.

Jazz purists cringe at her parodies, impersonations and foot stomping, but few fault her pianistic talents. Chastisements about her stage behavior don't seem to bother Dorothy, as long as her fans love her. She just keeps delivering her high-energy performances in her own inimitable way.

Toshiko Akiyoshi

Toshiko was born in Manchuria and began her piano studies while young. Later her family moved to Japan where she had access to records, especially those of Bud Powell, which directed her interests to improvisation. Then in the early 1950's, Oscar Peterson visited a Tokyo jazz club and heard her play. His recommendation to Norman Granz resulted in a recording session. After moving to the United

States a few years later, Toshiko studied in Boston and formed her own group. While working with trios and small combos, she began to gravitate toward composing for a larger band. In 1972 she and her husband, a tenor sax and flute player, formed the Toshiko Akiyoshi-Lew Tabackin Big Band. As composer-arranger and conductor of the 16-piece all male band, her talents have gained wide recognition. Face hidden by long dark hair which hung to the keyboard, Toshiko performed with the band at the first Kansas City Women's Jazz Festival in 1978. The band was named the top big-band by *Downbeat's* Reader Poll in 1978 and has enjoyed continued popularity at concerts such as their Town Hall appearance in March of 1982.

Toshiko has made a unique contribution to modern jazz by her ability to blend traditional sounds of the Orient with modern western idioms. "Minimata," a four-part suite portrays musically the small Japanese fishing village that was contaminated by mercury poisoning. "Yellow is Mellow" is another of her well-known compositions. Her piano work, sometimes hard and driving, has caused fellow musicians to comment that she has more guts than any man when she performs. Leonard Feather called her playing "fiery, powerfully articulated and exceptionally fluent." The tiny composer has traveled to Japan several times to work with musicians there. Toshiko continues to flavor her compositions with musical memories of her heritage and contributes another page of history to the world of jazz.

[1]Stephen Holden, *The New York Times*, October 9, 1981, p.22.

VIII

Pianists of the Heartland

Jazz spent its adolescence in the Midwest. After its infancy in Louisiana, jazz meandered up the Mississippi River and its tributaries, spreading joy to all who listened. The art form was modified along the way, generating the popular Kansas City and Chicago styles. Today the inland states offer jazz of every persuasion in settings ranging from riverboats to concert halls. The following women are examples of the many excellent female keyboard artists throughout the country who play jazz.

Lorna Michaelson

Lorna has been performing in Europe and the Far East since 1978; between engagements, she returns to Minneapolis to relax and visit friends. Her multifaceted background includes recording, radio and television, symphony experience, dance, astrology, and the title of Miss North Dakota in a Miss America Contest. "I constantly consider doing other things," she said. "Plumbing, teaching, traveling, writing ... almost anything to get away from the pressure." However, there are no signs that music is easing its grip on the pianist who recently returned from an extensive tour which terminated in Hong Kong. She prefers staying for long periods of time while playing in other countries. "That way I can learn the culture," she said. "I eat the food, go to concerts, learn the music. I do love to travel."

Additions to her repertoire of ethnic dances are another advantage of her wanderlust. While in Beirut, she studied the art of Arabic dance and on the island of Majorca, she learned flamenco dancing. Following her experiences in the Middle East, she opened her own

Lorna Michaelson.

dance and music studio in Minneapolis. During her stay in Hong Kong, Lorna taped interviews with career women and made travelogue-type tapes to be broadcast to Midwest audiences in the U.S. However far from home, she doesn't forget her roots.

At the age of four Lorna began playing the piano under the tutelage of Belle Mehus, whom she credits with giving her a solid musical foundation. (Her teenaged daughters Julie and Maria also studied with Ms. Mehus and have presented recitals with their mother.) Lorna went on to receive scholarships to the Conservatories of Music in Chicago and Los Angeles and the Mannes School of Music in New York. While in high school, Lorna was hired to play classical music on KFYR radio three times a day. The money she earned was spent on clothes and concerts when she later attended school in Chicago. One of her first jobs after that was playing with a quartet that included a guitar player who "made life hell on stage." So she is grateful the other two in the group protected her and helped her learn.

She fell in love with the sound of jazz, its harmonies, its freedom and joy. The decision to make it her livelihood seemed natural when she was faced with raising her daughters alone, though at times she misses the classics which she studied for years. "The only discouragement I ever felt was from inside myself," she said. "I had so much to learn in the repertoire that it was study and listen, or learn and play songs immediately." Two pianists Lorna admires are Jeanne Arland Peterson ("She plays like a dynamo and has good sound and technique") and Dave Brubeck ("He uses only the important notes and harmonies and doesn't embroider too much"). One of her favorite memories is a recent performance of Brubeck's "Brandenburg Gate" with an orchestra.

The musician has been engaged by over a dozen American hotel chains over the years. She's appeared at the Tyrone Guthrie Theatre and the Museum of Art in Minneapolis. Lorna was a musical instructor at the American University in Beirut and has taught jazz history, concepts, and harmonies at the MacPhail Center for the Performing Arts at the University of Minnesota and at the University of Arkansas. "Many first-rate musicians gave lectures and shared their expertise with my students during those courses," she said. "It is difficult to teach 'whole music' and to turn out 'whole musicians.'"

Lorna points out that "all periods of classical music went through difficult times," and she sees "jazz as just one more form that has to fight for its right to be heard and kept as a legitimate form." She maintains that musicians of the United States and Canada are better trained and more qualified than in any other area in the world. She also feels American teaching methods are far superior to all others.

Women entering the music field would be better prepared by taking courses on how to manage their money, time and talents, the keyboard artist advised. Mismanagement of her talent and money proved to be a major problem. "It's a shame that musicians often are rewarded by the amount of publicity that is pumped out about them," she said. "Many times the best musicians don't receive commensurate pay and recognition because they lack the drive of the lesser talented who are better managers."

"Lorna's Here" is the title of her album and also of a late-night television show which the musician had in the 1970's. Her love of astrology led her to present musical horoscopes for her audiences. This successful series was later shown on Monte Carlo English television. Lorna recently initiated yet another way to blend her musical and astrological talents. She develops and presents V.I.P. Musical Horoscopes to honor individuals of companies, associations and clubs. After the awards program or party, a picture album and cassette tape of the event are given to the guest-of-honor.

Among the least desirable aspects of Lorna's work are not being paid enough for what she does, and continually being asked to "do me a favor," by playing for nothing or by giving free lessons. Whether sitting down at a piano in Zurich, Hong Kong or her home town, she is quite serious about her profession and women musicians who occasionally share the stage with her. "I'm always very proud of the women and have great feelings about them," Lorna said. "They are marvelously talented and inspiring!"

Nadine Jansen

Rex Reed described Nadine Jansen as a musician "who plays four keyboards with her left hand while she plays trumpet and flugelhorn with her right hand. Damnedest thing I've ever seen. She plays like Shorty Rogers, except he needs two hands."[1] Sometimes known as "The Queen of Jazz" in western circles, six-foot-tall Nadine Jansen has been a professional musician for over thirty years and has weathered occupational hazards ranging from falling off a stage and breaking her elbow to having her tooth chipped when a man hit the end of her flugelhorn and said, "Women don't do that, so throw it out."

The multitalented musician is primarily a pianist who, at the age of four, first started playing by ear the songs she heard on the radio. Classical training followed, but she always was drawn back to jazz. "My 18 years of classical training was an advantage in every way," she said. "It gave me technique, ear training and enabled me to execute ideas." After graduating from high school at the age of fifteen, Nadine entered San Jose State College. It was during this time that her brother-in-law encouraged her interest in jazz with his collection of records. In 1948 she auditioned for Horace Heidt and was hired for his band, traveling with his group for three years. They did five vaudeville shows a day between films in movie houses. Nadine entertained alongside Rosemary and Betty Clooney and Dick Contino. After that she was sent out on a road show with a comedian who complained to their agent, "She can't walk and only has one evening gown." His attitude shattered Nadine's confidence so much, she tried to sneak on and off the stage so no one would notice her. Before long she began appearing as a single in small clubs, at one time alternating with Charlie Parker.

Becoming an Army wife while still quite young didn't work out. She couldn't adjust to Army living. So after her husband's term was up, they tried the entertainment circuit together (he played drums). That didn't work either, so he eventually returned to the Army.

Nadine continued to perform and learned how to deal with club owners, developing tolerance along the way. There were times she was ordered by agents to "strip, sing or get off the stage." The statuesque Scandinavian first worked in the Valley in 1958 when she was booked into the Pump Room in Phoenix. Then she moved to the Band Box,

Nadine Jansen.

which was in need of a Dixieland pianist for its band. She played there on and off for eight years. Guest performers included Paul Horn, Stuff Smith, Buddy Collette and Shorty Rogers. Steady bookings in Scottsdale followed. Nadine received encouragement from other musicians, Charlie Teagarden saying she was a "marvelous musician and entertainer" and Pete Jolly considering her "very versatile and talented."

One of her favorite pianists is Marian McPartland, who has been supportive. "She knows the instrument so thoroughly and is able to play brilliant chord changes in any key," Nadine said. "She came to my home and I played flugelhorn with her and then keyboards. She encouraged me to audition for the Kansas City Jazz Festival."

One high point in Nadine's career occured in Scottsdale, Arizona. "I organized a three day mini-festival with Pete Jolly and his trio plus my trio. We alternated and while I sat in on flugelhorn, Kai Winding showed up. I never blew better — got a standing ovation."

Nadine later teamed up with guitar-vocalist Mary Kaye for engagements in Las Vegas and California. Mary Kaye was the second female vocalist to be named to the American Jazz Hall of Fame. The first was Ella Fitzgerald. In 1978 the Mary Kaye/Nadine Jansen Quartet opened the new Casbah in Las Vegas with Don Rickles and were voted one of the top five performing groups by the Academy of Variety and Cabaret Acts. That same year they received rave reviews in *The*

New York Times during their three-month stint at the Montauk Yacht Club. They were lauded for their intensity and versatility in performing hard-driving, syncopated bop, progressive jazz and pop tunes.

Her signature piece, "Green Dolphin Street" is a favorite with her audience, with whom she creates a warm rapport. "I try to get across what I'm feeling," she said, "so that others can also feel it." Being an entertainer requires strength, and Nadine finds that is one of her problems as a woman musician. "It's difficult dealing with the image people have that strength detracts from your sexuality. It's just not true. I've never tried to play like a man, just as a person." Her unusual ability to play piano and flugelhorn simultaneously while sitting at the piano demands considerable strength, but she's been doing it so long, she doesn't even think about it.

When she was twelve she studied the trumpet, and her sister accompanied her on piano. One day Nadine got frustrated that her sister couldn't play in a jazz style. "You don't swing," she told her. "I'll do it myself." Years later, Nadine is still "doing it herself," with neither instrument being slighted. She also vocalizes in a husky voice. For relaxation she sometimes loads up her keyboard equipment and Siamese cats in her van and goes camping, but she always returns to ardent fans in the Scottsdale area where she has made her home. Herb Johnson, the founder of Jazz in Az, always welcomes Nadine back. "She is great, so magnificent," he said of his longtime friend.

Nadine had two records released, both on her own label, and she wrote most of the sound score for the movie *Grad Night*. She has compiled a series of songs with narration for a children's album and teaches piano part-time at the Bob Ravenscroft Music Studio in Scottsdale. "I think the future for jazz and women musicians looks great, and I want to help as much as I can," she said. "We should go back to playing from the heart instead of trying to outplay each other technically. We need more togetherness."

Frances Campbell

Frances enjoyed watching old silent movies as a young girl. The wonderful sounds that emanated from the movie house piano made such an impression on her, she decided to become a pianist. Later on, as she met other musicians, she settled into jazz. Lil Hardin, Norma Teagarden and Marian McPartland were women she admired for their faculties at the keyboard. She also mentioned Don Ewell, Gene

Frances Campbell.

Schroeder (with whom she played duets), Earl Hines, Clayton Richie, Dave Bowman and Ralph Sutton as masters of jazz piano. Frances's experiences over the years include working with Ralph Sutton, Pee Wee Hunt, Preacher Rollo and the Saints. She also played intermission piano for Jack Teagarden, Don Ewell and the World's Greatest Jazz Band. The pleasant soft-featured pianist now resides in Wisconsin Dells, a popular Wisconsin resort area, where she and her husband Herb play in jazz groups and dance bands. The past several summers have been spent aboard the Clipper Winnebago, playing the organ while the boat cruises up and down the river.

"I began playing when I was four," she said. "I had no classical training at all." She can remember sitting on several thick books in order to reach the keys. Her exceptional talent, creativity and determination enabled her to teach herself to play. By the time she was 13, she was playing professionally. The next few years she filled solo engagements and did radio broadcasts. It was during one of the radio shows that a tuba/trombone player with a band in Madison, Wisconsin, heard the young pianist. "That was some of the best jazz piano I'd ever heard," Herb Campbell later recalled. When Frances' name was

announced, he realized that he remembered her from his youth in
Wisconsin Dells. Their friendship was rekindled and within a short
time, they were married. That was in 1937.

Herb had played with a dance band when he was very young,
and later worked in the bands of Bob Crosby, Bunny Berigan, Gene
Krupa and other top musicians, sometimes with Frances at his side. "I
worked as a single for many years," said Frances, who performed quite
often in Florida. "Nearly all of the work we did together was in the
bands." The couple traveled thousands of miles while touring the country during the big band era. They performed in cities from New York
to San Francisco, as well as many out-of-the-way places. Band dates in
New Orleans meant all-night jam sessions and a myriad of pioneer jazz
greats to listen to. Herb and Frances could never get enough of the
music. Whenever their schedule permitted, they returned to their
hometown on the Wisconsin River. There they could enjoy their friends
in a tranquil environment until job commitments took them back
out on the road again. When they retired, the two musicians formed
their own band to play around the Dells area. Alto sax man Boyce
Brown and Tommy Thuenen, who played trumpet, were members of
their band, as well as some of the top local musicians. "We had some
happy times," she said.

Frances and her husband participate every year at the annual
Bix Biederbecke Festival in Davenport, Iowa, and the Bunny Berigan
Festival at nearby Fox Lake. The performer's vibrant Dixieland piano
has been heard in nearly every supper club within miles. She especially
favors playing in the style of Pinetop Smith and Fats Waller and feels
their music can never be improved upon through experimentation. "I
play for my own satisfaction as well as to please others," the accomplished musician said. "I've never regretted my life as a pianist and
would be destroyed if I couldn't continue to play."

Claudia Burson

Claudia has been a professional musician since her high school
days, but had to face reality about supporting herself solely through
her music. She works in an office in Houston and plays piano evenings
and weekends on whatever jobs are available. "Country-western is big
in Houston," she said. "During the mid-1970's there seemed to be a
resurgence of jazz, but now you have to search for it." She has no

agent, so relies on others' referrals. The pianist has found the musical community around the Houston area to be supportive. "That's what keeps us alive," she admitted.

After studying classical music at the University of Arkansas and the Berklee School of Music in Boston, Claudia was away from music for a time, but was drawn back in the early 1970's. By that time she found she had acquired bad habits and needed help with her technique. She relied on Beatriz J. Pilapil to get her back on the track. "She was a dynamic teacher," Claudia said. "She really helped me develop speed and clarity through proper scale practice. The classics are definitely beneficial."

The musician has since played in small clubs and for private functions. After participating in an Austin concert, she drew strength from the women's community of musicians and made new friends. She appears regularly with vocalist Horace Grigsby's combo and teams up with a bass player from Austin for duo work. "Women in Jazz" was the theme for one six-week engagement in Austin. The five-piece band was organized by photographer Patti Polinard who wrote up their résumés and did the photography for the group's publicity. They entertained at Lakewood and then were booked into the Sheraton-Hilton. "Each of us had a different woman artist to research for the program," Claudia said. "We had trouble finding material on them, but we did the best we could and were well received." Though playing only jazz isn't always possible, the pianist tries to arrive at a compromise so that she can play some of her own tunes as well as those the club managements prefer. Her pet peeve is the out-of-control patron who annoys the musicians and stumbles over the band's equipment.

Mary Lou Williams, Marian McPartland and Shirley Scott are the women she most admires for their keyboard style. She felt that Marian McPartland's workshop at a Kansas City Women's Jazz Festival had been helpful to her. "I grew up in the swing era," she said. "I like blues, and straight ahead sound with a lot of improvisation, and all original music. We've been trying to get a Sunday gig going so we can play what we like. Even if the money's not there, it's still worth doing."

Claudia was made aware of talent in the Houston area when she was invited to play at a band competition judged by tenor saxophonist Don Wilkinson and other name musicians. "The kids played great," she said. "I just hope the demand will support their talents if they make the decision to work in such an insecure profession."

Claudia's future plans include going to New York, but she won't risk it unless she has a good engagement or substantial savings. She has considered other avenues in the field of music and has added teaching to her already busy life. Her students are learning theory and jazz improvisation as well as the classics. Claudia draws and paints for relaxation and has taken up photography as a hobby. Creativity is very important to her, and she expresses it in different ways, though her first love is playing her own original music.

Her only brush with discrimination came when she inquired about a job in a cocktail lounge duo. The manager turned her down without listening to her play because he'd already hired one woman and didn't want two. "You just have to maintain a positive attitude," she said of the disappointment.

Bonnie G. Fuqua

Though Bonnie G, as she is called professionally, began "playing and improvising" while sitting on her father's knee, she didn't become a jazz pianist until many years later. The entertainer first had a career in radio broadcasting. She was a news announcer, worked in radio and TV advertising and played as a studio pianist. "Through my years in radio and TV, while accompanying singers and joining jam sessions, I always found good fellowship among musicians," she said. Going out on her own seemed a natural transition. Bonnie is now a solo pianist/vocalist appearing at Sheratons and other motel and hotel chains. She feels her music has never let her down. "I believe it is a God-given talent," she said, "and I was fortunate to have loving and intelligent parents who recognized and guided this talent through the formative years. Later they were financially able to afford very good training for me. It's always been a labor of love and fulfillment. I know I've been lucky, and I'm grateful."

She was sometimes let down by circumstances, however, such as the time she received a letter of commendation and praise from the management of a club. The last paragraph stated that "All good things must come to an end," thus terminating her contract. There were pleasant surprises along the way too. Once she arrived for an eight-week engagement at a club and discovered that she was to replace her idol Teddy Williams who had been appearing as featured performer. "Finding a style brings individual recognition for a pianist," Bonnie said, "and to be a crowd pleasing performer, I often have to 'switch gears' instantly." Bonnie feels each piano has a "soul" of its own — which she feels she must explore in order to achieve harmony during a performance. "I'm a purist," she admitted. "In my opinion, 'too busy' or 'too far out' is a distraction. Getting carried away by one's own technical brilliance destroys the musical themes and ends up as a conglomeration of nothing."

What does the Shreveport, Louisiana, pianist strive for in her music? "Perfection — as I hear it."

Iris Bell

Raising beef cattle and Siamese cats, selling real estate, turning her farm into campsites — these are options Iris Bell considers from time to time. But a flashback to Mr. Kelly's in Chicago makes them vanish. The pianist/singer needs only remember following comedian Freddie Prinze at the popular club. "It had been my dream to play Mr. Kelly's, where all the living jazz greats had played," she said. "I walked on that stage with the greatest feeling of exaltation I'd ever experienced."

From early on, an extraordinary ear for harmony and an excellent feel for rhythm made Iris a fast learner. She now admits she was lazy about her lessons and less than thrilled at deciphering classical music. George Shearing's mastery of the keyboard impressed her so much, she made the decision to pursue jazz at the age of 14. "I wish I had had teachers who knew how to polish my various facets," she said. "What I acquired, I had to get by listening and trying. There is no magic. You must practice, practice, practice! And listen only to the best, then devote whatever time it takes to be *better* than the best you ever heard. It's important to strive to create something none of your influences has ever played." It would have been easy to pander to audiences who didn't understand, but Iris wanted to perform jazz for aficionados only. In spite of the dearth of jobs, Iris did make it. Her first job was playing and singing for a black chapter of Shrine, playing mostly rhythm and blues ("Honey Hush," "Shake, Rattle and Roll," etc.) After taxes were deducted, she made $8.30. "During that gig, I was handed an enormous cup of whisky, the first I'd seen," she recalled. "I thought I was supposed to drink it all! After the intermission, I couldn't find middle C, but I learned not to drink and play."

The young blond musician was named winner of a contest in 1954 by Lionel Hampton. She then played and sang "Midnight Sun" with his band at Castle Farm, a 2,000 seat nightclub in Cincinnati. Iris was grateful for his assistance and has since tried to help younger

Iris Bell.

musicians by writing out charts and recommending ways to improve their performances.

Besides performing and composing (her tune "I Hear Him Comin' Down the Road" was recorded on the Warner Brothers label), Iris was a music critic for *The Charleston Gazette* for some time. One of her most enjoyable assignments was interviewing and writing a review on Chris Connor at a recent West Virginia Jazz Festival. Iris herself has been featured on that program every year since 1978. In 1982, The Iris Bell Adventure played the final evening of the popular five-day jazz festival, sharing the stage with the Dukes of Dixieland. She has also appeared at the National Women's Music Festival in Champaign-Urbana, Illinois. Melissa Manchester and Billy Preston are among the top names she's worked with at concerts and on night club tours.

Iris recalled one evening she'll never forget. An outdoor concert in 1970 was attended by the pianist's elderly mother, who hadn't heard her daughter play for several years. She was enjoying Iris's performance from her seat at the side of the stage when right at her feet, two dogs became vigorously amorous. "My mother lost interest in me," Iris laughed. "She began beating the dogs with her umbrella, shrieking 'Stop it! Stop it!'"

Iris's regimen calls for no smoking or late hours and little drinking. When not working, she recharges herself with good reading, records and conversation. Another pleasant diversion is gardening.

The shortage of good accompanists in the beginning of her musical career led Iris to develop her own piano style, and now she favors pianistically-oriented tunes, percussive tunes and seldom heard ballads. Some of her all-time favorites are "Never Will I Marry," "Red Clay," "There Will Never Be Another You," "Maiden Voyage" and "Sidney's Soliloquy."

Being a woman has been more of a help than a detriment, the musician feels. "However, you have to be so good that nobody can accuse you of getting by *because* you're female!"

According to Iris, an enormous role reversal has taken place, with males appearing to be less aggressive and women more adventurous. "I figure women will utilize their bent for logic to explore their ability to compute like machines, and their intuition and soul to make improvisation appealing to the emotions."

Sometimes Iris finds playing the piano is absolutely effortless, as though the hands act independently of the brain. "There is such an intense connection between the chord changes and the zillion possible ways to go improvisationally that no thought is necessary," she concluded.

Lovell Litton

After years of homemaking and parenting, Lovell Litton made the decision in 1978, at the urging of her husband, to become a professional jazz pianist. Since then she has led a Dixieland band and plays the country club circuit in and around Birmingham, Alabama, in a piano/bass duo. "I deeply regret that I didn't get really serious a lot sooner," she said. "I now approach my music with a near degree of fanaticism. I eat, drink, sleep and live music. My family has to understand that it is now 'time for me.'"

Lovell has had no problem receiving equal pay and has been hired for mostly "cream of the crop" engagements in Birmingham. She enjoys playing all types of music, except funk. The pianist thinks jazz would benefit from a pause in experimentation because she thinks there is nothing more to be said.

Though a career in jazz is demanding, Lovell said it's worth every effort. To her the future looks bright for women musicians though she warns them to expect to be severely judged. "I'm sort of racing against the clock since I waited so long to begin," she said. "Her new vocation presented situations she has never coped with before, like gettng out of the predicament of hiring two drummers for the same gig! She also admits there are things to be learned from listening to the younger generation. "My 28-year-old bass player feels free to point out weak areas in my playing," she said. "That makes me stop, reevaluate what I'm doing, and practice like hell!"

Lovell goes running two or three days a week to stay in shape. But what she loves most is practicing. Among her idols are Marian McPartland, Patrice Rushen, Art Tatum, Bud Powell, Bill Evans, Joe Sample, Toshiko Akiyoshi and McCoy Tyner. "I hope to sound like a composite of them in the not-too-distant future," she said. The musician was greatly honored recently when invited to participate as the featured artist with the jazz consort from the Birmingham Symphony Orchestra in concert in Decatur, Alabama. Music is her life now and she won't consider doing anything else. "I think this is the ultimate channel of self expression," she said. "When I'm playing my best, I feel as close to heaven as walking in the door."

Beth Brown

"I was discouraged by circumstances, men and institutions," Beth said of her early inclinations to play jazz. That did not stop her from realizing her dreams. She taught piano to young students to help pay her way through Bryn Mawr College from which she received a degree in music composition. At times during her senior year, her infant son accompanied her to class! She also studied privately with Vladimir Sokoloff and Agi Jambor. Otis Brown, a performing poet, provided motivation and understanding. She was determined not to let herself feel limited by the environment. But the lack of good jobs, equal pay and respect for her as a professional artist is sometimes disheartening. "I intend to keep practicing, writing and performing, though," she said. "Music is one of my loves, and I would feel terribly deprived if I didn't play."

The pianist also cites the commercialism of the music scene and the absence of recording opportunities as two serious problems. She feels that taking advantage of some of the excellent workshops in performing and recording skills is a good way to meet peers and make connections that may lead to work. The musicians she most respects are Carla Bley, Chick Corea, Bill Evans, Phillip Glass ("He contributes to our understanding of the world of sound, both natural and man-made") and McCoy Tyner ("for his enchanted fluid style").

Beth feels jazz must be seen by an international point of view in the future. "There are a number of European groups that have caught the spirit of American and Afro-American music of the 1940's and 1950's" she remarked. "They are advancing the music we lost to fancy technologies."

Beth has performed in Philadelphia and New York and along the East Coast. She has done studio work and played at Afro-American cultural events and at festivals. A flutist named Mojo collaborated with Beth, who feels they both found encouragement from their non-competitive association. The young pianist will never forget the thrill of receiving a fellowship from the CBS Foundation to study writing and communications at the University of Pennsylvania. "Improvisation is an experiment," she said, "but writing music enters several other dimensions. When I'm not in school, studying or playing, I write." She is influenced by the compositions of Antonio Carlos Jobim of Brazil and the minimalist tradition. Beth feels her compositions are becoming more important to making a world of musical symbols in which she can explore. "Only by creating a sense of well-being through music, can one reap the benefit of self knowledge," she concluded. "I plan to remain within my world of symbolism and sound."

Nancy Marshall

"I've always known that music was the one thing no one could take away from me," Nancy said. "If I couldn't play, I'd sing. If I couldn't sing, I'd bang on a drum." Studying classical music from her early childhood through college because she had no choice, she finally learned the basics of jazz through Bert Konowitz's books and workshops, and she is still evolving as a jazz pianist. Her career choice met with pessimism all around. "I was discouraged in every way," she said. "The culture told me I should be a wife and mother, the schools I attended told me they couldn't teach me jazz, and the first person I married insisted I didn't know how to play jazz." Nancy finds it a struggle to succeed as a jazz artist in Lincoln, Nebraska, where work involving real jazz is scarce. She once considered becoming a court reporter, but decided to rely on a three-fold teaching job to make enough money so she can afford to play the music she loves. She teaches music in her home, at a preschool, and at a daycare center.

Playing in mostly entertainment-type shows since high school, Nancy first worked with a regular jazz group just a few years ago. The

Nancy Marshall.

money she earned that summer was spent on carpeting for her family room. The most encouragement she's received came from the musicians' union president who helped her find a niche in the Lincoln music scene. She's worked with her own trio and with Blue Wave, J.P. Quint, and the Lincoln Jazz Society. "I've played in every bar in town that hires jazz pianists," Nancy stated. "It's disappointing that so few people really appreciate jazz. When we go out and play, some fool always asks, 'Don't you know any disco?' To have something you dearly love continually rejected, really hurts."

Nancy's family is supportive and her sessions on the racquetball court help her stay fit and release tensions. Her sense of humor takes the sting out of unpleasant incidents like the one that occurred in Alexandria, Nebraska, "a one-street town." She was to sing and play electric piano on a solo gig. "The first hint that I was in trouble came when I saw signs that read 'Nancy Marshall and her electric piano will play your favorite songs,' " she said. "They kept requesting things like 'Cab Driver!' I didn't know 'Cab Driver!' I did manage to pull off some golden oldies like 'San Antonio Rose,' but early into the second set, the manager told me he didn't think it was working out and I could leave if I wanted to, and he'd still pay the full amount. I told him I'd be glad to stay and play out the gig. The second hint that they didn't want me to stay was when the manager handed out quarters to his friends to play the juke box. My third hint was when an unattractive man came over and said, 'You play real nice, but when you sing, something just happens.' I didn't think he meant it as a compliment." Nancy made the best of a bad experience and composed a blues tune about that ego-shattering night. She still loves to sing it!

The pianist appreciates Mary Lou Williams' bluesy elegance, Oscar Peterson ("his three-handed style, the gospel licks, the runs, my God, the man!"), Thelonious Monk, Marian McPartland and Bill Evans. The biggest thrill of her career came when she forced herself to get up on the stage and play at the Women's Jazz Festival in Kansas City, even though she didn't feel she was good enough. "I felt about 200 feet tall for months," she remembered, "and it helped me get back to Lincoln and hustle some more gigs."

When Nancy is playing her very best, she feels fantastic, gets goose bumps, and the hair stands up on her arms. She admits it's a good thing she doesn't always play her best. "I couldn't stand the ecstasy!"

Mary Jane Brown

While growing up in Detroit, Mary Jane Brown knew she would be a jazz pianist. "There was an innate feeling from the beginning," she said. Listening to the music of Art Tatum, Fats Waller, Mary Lou Williams, Oscar Peterson and Hazel Scott was a favorite pastime of hers. "I still think the music from the 1930's and 1940's is the greatest," she stated. Most of her 35 years in the business have been spent working solo in Detroit and touring with her own group throughout the Northwest. But for the last 15 years she has been playing with a congenial six-piece group, the Bourbon Street Dixieland Jazz Band. The group provides entertainment at various jazz spots in southern Arizona. Mary Jane is the only woman in the band and is grateful that her colleagues continually cheer her on, as other musicians have all her life. That is important to her since she wants to perform better on each job she plays. She thinks every jazz musician can benefit from playing Bach and must be ready for anything whether appearing as a single or with a band.

Only on one occasion did she have the opportunity to play with other female musicians. "I enjoyed it," she said of the experience. "It was a small group with two good horns." Feeling music knows no gender, Mary Jane said the future is wide open for women and the only way to go is *up*. Her advice is, "Go, girl! And never quit practicing!" The fact that age doesn't limit a good musician wasn't left unmentioned by the enthusiastic pianist. "I've reached my 60's" she said, "and I play with the finest band in the territory."

Unforgettable events during her long and successful career include the first time she saw her name in lights, the Bob Hope Show she played for and a performance for President Eisenhower. "I was very disappointed, though, when I wasn't able to go overseas with the USO during World War II," she admitted. But the congenial woman is thankful she was able to follow her dream of becoming a professional Dixieland pianist. Mary Jane is content with her life and wouldn't trade her experiences with anyone. "If I couldn't play the piano, I'd flip out," she said.

Judy Strauss

Judy knows she's playing her best when she is totally immersed in the music, yet aware that her listeners are tapping their feet and keeping time with their bodies. "I feel like smiling, especially at the rest of the group," the slender brunette said. But the Cleveland musician doesn't work as often as she would like and through the years has had to supplement her income in other ways. Several years ago she took a local pianist's advice and started teaching. Since then she has derived most of her support from that, still performing though whenever she gets the chance. She has worked in trios such as Potology, which performs mainstream jazz, and has her own five-piece combo, The Music Minority. Judy has led the latter group at Hollenden House Hotel, El Morocco, Native Son Lounge, Park Plaza Hotel, Harley Hotel, Plato's Place, Clifton Club and other local establishments. They've also appeared at museum-sponsored festivals and played for corporate dinner dances.

In late 1977, the Northeast Ohio Jazz Society was founded by writers and broadcasters to promote jazz in the Greater Cleveland area. To foster awareness of the music and to provide scholarships for the study of jazz, a series of fund-raising concerts were presented. Judy Strauss and the Music Minority performed at the first concert, which took place at Cleveland State University and was co-sponsored by the school's department of Black Studies. Later they were featured at several Music on the Mall concerts (1978-79) which were sponsored by the city and the Cleveland Federation of Musicians. The Metro Campus Auditorium was the setting for "Jazz in Concert," presented in the spring of 1982. The Music Minority and the Stablemates Quintet pooled their talents to entertain in the jazz idiom to benefit the college's

Judy Strauss. (Photo by Madison Geddes.)

food task force. In addition Judy has appeared at concerts featuring Cannonball Adderly and Shirley Scott. She's also been a featured guest on the television show, "Montage," during which she and bass player Ola White performed and discussed women's role in jazz.

The musician improvised from the first time she sat down at the piano. Classical training built up her technique and reading abilities. At 15 she began listening to her older brother's Dave Brubeck records which led to her decision to become a jazz pianist. "A bandleader and booker told me 20 years ago that I'd never make any money at it," she recalled. "My parents weren't too happy about some of the places I played, either." She continued, "On one of my first jobs, we made the mistake of accepting a percentage of the night's receipts instead of a set fee." "Needless to say, we didn't make much!"

Judy could make more money playing commerical music, but just doesn't enjoy it. She prefers bop, bossa novas with good chord changes and ballads with a pretty melody and interesting chords. Because she leads her own group, she seldom gets calls as a sideman. Her main problems are club owners who don't always take her seriously as a musician and the electric keyboard equipment she has to lug around. "I find the competitiveness of the music business discouraging," she also admitted. "I don't like trying to talk club owners into hiring my band. Some musicians are willing to work for peanuts which makes it harder for those of us who want a decent wage. Around this area, good bookers for jazz jobs are scarce and club owners are poor about publicizing their bands, so we end up doing it ourselves."

Judy has worked with women bass players, singers and drummers. She listens to the recordings of Barbara Carroll, Marian McPartland, and Joanne Grauer. "Generally, I find men's playing more heavily rhythmic and women's more introspective," she said.

The pianist's practice sessions begin with exercises and then proceed to the current repertoire. During her free time, Judy attends classical and jazz concerts, art shows and the ballet. She swims, walks, plays Ping-Pong and badminton to stay in shape. When told how well she plays for a woman, she answers, "I know I play as well as a lot of men and better than some!"

Phyllis Fabry

"I'm glad I'm a woman," Phyllis said. "When you play well, sex doesn't matter. You're part of it all!" The ability to play by ear was put to the test early in Phyllis' life when she was hired to play jazz on a radio show at the age of seven. She can't remember what she played, but that was the first of many performances on radio and TV for the pianist-organist. She has entertained throughout the United States and in Africa and Europe, where she was offered a good job traveling with a jazz band throughout England, Scotland and Ireland. "I've always put my family first," the Peoria musician said. "Consequently, my career in the past has been limited to my home area except for a couple of weeks a year." Her husband and six children are all musically talented.

She studied the classics for 18 years and loved to practice, but was discouraged from making a career in the classical field, so she turned to jazz. Her years of training honed her technique and ear training, but she found it also could confine creativity if a musician wasn't alert. Studying with Miss Schneidman, a classical pianist from Vienna, made a lasting impression on Phyllis as a young woman. She credits the teacher for her generous encouragement and valuable instruction which has guided her over the years. "She was fantastic," Phyllis remembered.

Equally accepted by both women and men jazz musicians, she feels talent for jazz is the necessary ingredient for success. She is an admirer of Erroll Garner, Peter Nero and George Shearing, and has been told many times that her style resembles Marian McPartland's. "I play the way I play because I have to," she said. "I never play a piece exactly the same because I never feel the same." Her goal while performing is to bring others along on her musical journeys. Music is a part of her which she wishes to share with others. Phyllis fears that the "soul" of jazz could be lost through too much experimentation. "If we lose the music along the way, we may end up playing only for other musicians who can understand what we're doing technically," she said. "I would hate to see that happen."

Musicians from the Ellington and Dorsey bands sometimes worked the same clubs and sat in with Phyllis. Carmen McCrae and other singers used to drop by to sing a few songs. "That was complimentary to me as a pianist," she said. Her life as a keyboard entertainer has not been free of frustration, however. She thinks being in the right place at the right time can make a difference in an artist's career. "I'm disappointed when I hear a musician who is recording (with the best equipment and back-up musicians) and I know I'm better," she said. "I think I'm pretty lucky, though," Phyllis said. "I've had my family and music too." The ultimate compliment came late one night: another pianist came over to the piano and said, "Lady, you have a beautiful soul!" She replied, "What more can I ask for?"

Carol Flamm

Children in Columbus, Ohio, have the unique privilege of hearing music written and performed by women because Carol Flamm formed a women's music group which plays for school children under the auspices of the Artists in the Schools Program. The students are exposed to the music of women composers in twentieth century America. Performing with other women has always been a joy to Carol, who remembers the first time she was part of such a group. "I was just starting," she recalled. "We didn't feel so intimidated just playing with each other. It was wonderful." Her first job was singing in a chorus for a Rosh Hashanah (Jewish New Year) service. She was attending Ohio State University and hadn't the slightest idea of becoming a professional musician, a calling which generates ambivalent feelings in her.

Up until about five years ago Carol used only her voice professionally. She sang with Jay Clayton's "Voice Group" in New York City and at different clubs. She also assisted at vocal workshops. "Then I decided that to really be a single, I should play the piano too," she said. "I felt insecure and was easily intimidated, but somehow I've stuck it out." Though she had gained reading ability and feel for the piano from her classical studies as a child, she feels she was badly taught and had to work very hard when she started playing again. "I never learned theory," she said. "A pianist friend, Ed Moed shared lots of amazing records, and my teacher Dave Wheeler laid out the basics for me. When I later attended a jazz camp, I received encouragement from those who heard me play. They said they heard good things and told me to keep going."

Since then Carol has played and sung in the Top 40 Band, several rehearsal jazz bands and other groups ranging from an octet to a big band. Her solo engagements are mostly at different restaurants where she performs dinner music and light jazz. The musician's repertoire depends on whether she is playing solo or in a group. She favors sambas or modal and up-tempo pieces when playing with a group. Jazz waltzes, ballads and swing tunes with interesting chord changes top her list of solo selections.

Carol appreciates the beautiful colors of McCoy Tyner's playing, the clear ideas of Wynton Kelly and the taste of Hank Jones. She finds it difficult to put into words her feelings when she is playing exceptionally well. "I see colors and space," she said, "and I experience such harmony between body and mind." For physical and mental relaxation, the musician likes to swim, read and dance. She enjoys cooking and mostly prepares health food dishes which she serves with tea.

Carol hopes for a greater integration of the masculine and feminine in the psyche of each individual. "Music can help women realize their power to create," she concluded, "and that will enable them to change the world into a more respected and loving place."

[1]Rex Reed, *Travolta to Keaton: Intimate Visits with Today's Top Superstars* (Berkley Books).

IX

East Coast Pianists

From the rocky shores of Maine to palm tree–lined beaches in Florida, the Eastern coastline is dotted with cities and resort areas that feature jazz as a staple entertainment. New York, the international center for jazz, attracts musicians who hope to gain recognition there. From North to South, there is an abundance of accomplished women pianists who have a common goal: to teach, to perform and to compose jazz.

Joanne Brackeen

Joanne recently articulated her feeling about music: "I don't consider music as a career — to me it is a necessity, just like breathing. We all know how to breathe from birth." When women pianists name their favorite peers, they invariably mention Joanne Brackeen. They admire her energy and her ability to express herself so forcefully, as well as her harmonic and rhythmic explorations. She is truly a "musician's musician." It was Leonard Feather who alerted jazz fans that she was the pianist to watch for in the 1980's. Her extensive recording and touring schedule both in the United States and abroad the past few years has borne out his predictions. Critics applaud her performances, and audiences increasingly respond to her vitalizing music.

Joanne began playing at the age of nine and is basically self-taught. When attending the Los Angeles Conservatory of Music on a scholarship, she lasted only three days. She didn't feel she was being taught music in a natural way. "I think real music comes from within oneself," she said, "and it should be taught from within. It is very important to recognize the inner energies and urges daily and put them

Joanne Brackeen. (Photo by Giuseppe Pino.)

directly into use in one's composing, improvising and daily living." Nat Hentoff has said of her playing, "There is this enormous authority. She *is* the music."

During the 1950's Joanne played on the West Coast with Dexter Gordon, Charles Lloyd, Bobby Hutcherson and other fine musicians. In 1960 she married saxophonist Charles Brackeen and within a few years had four children. Nonetheless she continued to play the piano

and compose, eventually returning to performing in 1965 when the
family moved to New York. She worked with Art Blakey for three
years, enjoyed a close musical association with saxophonist-composer
Joe Henderson and then joined Stan Getz's group. Joanne considers all
three men "musical masters." While with Getz, she recorded her first
album as a leader, a duo album with bassist Clint Houston, and a trio
record with both Houston and Billy Hart of Getz's rhythm section.

In 1977, Joanne struck out on her own and though she had no
plans on how to succeed as a solo, she received many calls for
engagements. "Some things just happen," Joanne said. More recordings
followed, she was a hit at the Berlin Jazz Festival, and *Down Beat's*
Critic's Poll placed her in the top ten. In 1978 bassist Eddie Gomez and
Joanne recorded a duo album, "Prism," which initiated a mutual
working coalition that has lasted through their most recent release of
"Special Identity." Drummer Jack DeJohnette joined them on the latter
recording of Joanne's original music. "It's an unbelievable help to have
someone to be able to hear and understand and play one's music in the
feeling out of which it was created," Joanne said. "Eddie Gomez, Jack
DeJohnette and Billy Hart have done this for me."

One of her compositions, "Einstein," doesn't have a key, set
measures, or chords. Yet her audiences don't consider it too "far out,"
perhaps because Joanne concentrates on awakening listeners so they
can feel what she feels. "Life gives you revelations and inspirations, and
they are phenomenal," she said. "In both my composition and improvisation, I express those inner feelings that reveal themselves to me
daily." No matter how complicated the passage, her playing never
sounds mushy. Each note is distinctly audible. Her physical strength
and acute musical emotions have made her unique. She feels that very
few musicians can play on the level necessary to really perform her
music adequately.

"I have no problem in being a woman musician," she said. "I
have always been accepted on an equal basis with men — in fact
usually far above." Joanne's future as a leading jazz artist looks impressive. She plays all the major jazz clubs and performs at jazz
festivals around the country. She sees more and more people respond-
ing to her music, and that excites her. She also has one wish to share
with others. "I would like every being in the universe to experience joy
forever."

Jane Jarvis

"I want to smell the roses. I want to play jazz from now on," Jane announced in 1978 when she left her position of vice-president at Muzak. The attractive keyboard artist has spent most of her life in music as a performer, composer, vocal coach, correspondent, arranger and record producer. "I always played jazz under a guise," she admitted. "If I'd announced myself as a jazz organist or jazz pianist, I'd never have gotten many of the jobs I played." Her decision to concentrate on jazz led to her becoming a member of the new Milt Hinton Trio which made its premiere performance at a concert in Northport, Long Island, on March 5, 1982. A short time later, Jane, Milt Hinton and Louis Bellson recorded an album. She also has teamed up with soprano saxman Bob Wilber to present jazz pipe-organ concerts at which they play traditional gospel hymns in jazz form. And she is a regular at Eddie Condon's in New York City with Ed Polcer and The Jam Preserve. Jane's abundant talent and energy are condensed into a trim 5' 1" body, which seems incongruous with the dynamic and harmonious effects she can produce while seated at a huge organ.

The musician was born in Vincennes, Indiana, and began playing the piano while very young. Her mother painted and had majored in drama and child psychology (then called behaviorism). She belonged to the school of prenatal thought and felt that anything she said, did or thought during pregnancy would have a vital impact on her child's behavior. "She was so enamored of music that she was certain I would be musical," Jane said, "even though there were no musicians on either side of the family. She wanted the best possible musical education for me."

Her mother came from a rigidly religious family. Smoking and drinking were unthinkable. "My grandfather told her he would give her an education if she promised never, never, never to play cards or dance," Jane said. "I guess she felt that wasn't giving up too much in her day and she agreed to it. She never danced, though she was cute and graceful, nor did she ever play cards." Jane's father was an attorney who wrote poetry and was generally credited with having written some of the first advertising jingles. For a hobby he wrote comedy-type verse for small newspapers. "He read literature to me as a child," Jane remembered, "and I think that's one of the reasons I can write lyrics with such consummate ease. I learned the rhythm of speech and the respect for speech that's needed in order to write."

Jane's mother didn't feel that her own promise to her father need

Jane Jarvis.

apply to her daughter. When nine-year-old Jane asked permission to
take dancing lessons, her mother was agreeable but asked how the girl
planned to pay for them. Her 25-cents allowance wouldn't go very
far. A series of lessons cost five dollars. "Looking back, I realize my
parents, who were far from poor, actually did me a favor," Jane said. "I
was so shy as a child. However, I did have this great belief in myself
musically. I don't think it made me stuck up but it did give me a wonderful secure feeling inside. I was scared to death, but I went to the
dancing teacher and asked to play piano in exchange for my lessons.
She was surprised at my proposal, but asked me to play, and then said
'yes.' Initially I played in exchange for the lessons. If I played every day
after school and on Saturdays for the other students, I could have one
private lesson and one class lesson a week. Well, my parents felt I was
being taken advantage of, so my mother said I had to go talk to her
again. I remember the icky feeling I had and the fear that I wouldn't be
able to continue my dancing. I went to see her and she agreed to pay
me ten cents an hour after I had worked out the two lessons."

Toward the end of the depression, Jane's family moved to Gary,
Indiana, where her father got a job with an insurance company, and
her mother taught school. Her mother was qualified to teach any sub-
ject in any of the twelve grades, except carpentry and music. When Jane
was ten she asked her father to take her to a radio kiddie show so she
could try out. She had her piano solos all ready—"Dizzy Fingers,"
"Nola" and similar flashy tunes so popular on kiddie shows at the time.
Some of the children arrived without an accompanist. The studio accompanist couldn't transpose so Jane, who was quite good at

transposing, was called upon to play for the other youngsters' singing and tap dancing. "I went there to play my own solo and ended up staying three or four hours," the pianist said. "At the end of the day, I was asked to come back every Saturday to work as the accompanist. For years I took it all for granted, but now being objective, I think it was remarkable. When I was 12 the radio station offered me a full-time job as official pianist. The catch was that I had to work after school until newstime, then accompany live programming from 7 p.m. to 10 p.m. I was offered $25 a week! This was at the end of the depression when a lot of married men considered themselves fortunate to be making $20 a week." Jane's mother recognized the opportunity and used her clout with friends in the school system. She arranged for her daughter to be excused from the first two hours of the morning classes so she'd get her rest. Eventually the schedule affected the girl's studies, so she worked only on Saturdays and joined a 12-piece band made up of high schoolers.

Jane's parents were killed in a train accident when she was 13. She had no brothers or sisters and shifted about with a number of relatives. "I think I weathered the terror of being left alone better than a lot of kids might have, by being allowed to have my first brush with business."

The first jazz tune Jane learned was "Don't Bring Me Posies, 'Cause It's Shoesies That I Need." Hearing the recorded playing of Jess Stacy and Teddy Wilson fanned her interest in jazz. One of her first appearances was with Eddie South, the "Dark Angel of the Violin." Jane bought a Hammond Organ so she would have an alternate means of support. When band jobs were scarce, she could usually find a hotel room that featured soloists. "There existed a social stigma to the word 'jazz,'" she said, "so I always referred to myself just as a musician. Had I announced myself as a jazz organist, I'd never have gotten the job playing organ at Shea Stadium. Nevertheless, I played jazz for 26 years—10 years for the Milwaukee Braves and 16 for the New York Mets."

Jane left a good job as staff pianist and organist at WTMJ in Milwaukee to go to New York City in 1963. She was surprised to find fewer women working there than in the Midwest. Finally hired as rehearsal and tryout pianist for the Johnny Carson Show, she worked for Skitch Henderson and later for Doc Severinson. Things looked rather bleak for pianists so Jane took a desk job at Muzak, figuring there might be a career for her within that organization. Through the recording sessions she met many major musicians in New York. "I bet on the right horse," she said of her decision. I became musical director and they kept giving me titles until they finally made me a vice-president." During the last ten years with Muzak, Jane produced over 300 albums, wrote and recorded over 300 tunes, was co-writer with Johnny Hodges, Steve Allen, Roy Eldridge, Bill Berry, Grady Tate, Clark Terry ("Clark's Bars") and Lionel Hampton ("Lionel's Train"). She also collaborated with her son on several jazz compositons. Her "Watch on the Rye," a riff-type tune, is still played by musicians in Milwaukee. Though she earlier had attended Bush Conservatory, the Chicago Conservatory and DePaul University School of Music, she returned to school and earned a degree in science from Pace University in 1977. During her years at Muzak, many awards came her way, but the one that meant the most came from a group of musicians in Buenos Aires. Through Jane they had done a great deal of recording and they gave her an attractive award. Even the union steward stamped it.

It was Lionel Hampton who first engaged Jane when she decided to perform again. It was also with Hampton that she hit the musical "high" of her career. She was producing a recording session with his 16-piece band (among the musicians were Richard Davis on bass, Bucky Pizzarelli on guitar and Grady Tate on drums). When the session was over, Hampton invited Jane to record a few tunes with the band. "He simply called the tunes and the key," Jane remembered. "I think that's the best I ever played in my life. That was a thrill!"

Flexibility has been a deciding factor in Jane's career, though she never accepted a job she wouldn't feel professional on, no matter how much money was involved. "The main reason I've made it is because I'm an 'ensemble thinker,'" she said. "Even though I occasionally miss a day at the piano, 75% of my waking hours are spent mentally reviewing music, and working out attitudes and postures. I never work out an arrangement on a tune to be played exactly the same way. If you're really a jazz musician, you can come up with a new idea every time you play. Tunes like 'Avalon' or 'Chinatown' leave little for a pianist to do because there's not enough harmonic interest. My recent favorites are 'How Long Has This Been Going On,' 'In Love in Vain' and everything by Hoagy Carmichael and Joe Henderson."

Jane admires Mary Lou Williams for being a complete musician, and Barbara Carroll and Marian McPartland for sustaining high professional standards. Singers Maxine Sullivan and Helen Humes (who died in 1981) are special to her. "Playing for them was like playing for horns," Jane said. "Helen was the more demanding, but probably didn't realize it. I was her friend and we both felt we sounded great together. Maxine sings fewer notes than anyone else and yet she can swing and swing hard. I love to play for her."

Most of Jane's musical associations have been with men and she has been accepted as an equal, though she feels men still prefer their own company in jazz. Woman must be exceptional in order to compete, and despite slow-going years ahead, she feels they will make it by virtue of numbers and quality. "Marriage is difficult, even if the woman does not fully pursue her career," she said. "Even for the most secure man, marriage to a musician presents problems. I'm not sure it can work."

Jane is a trustee of The House That Jazz Built, a member of the Universal Jazz Coalition and on the executive board of the International Art of Jazz, Inc., which maintains a year-round schedule of community concerts and arts-in-education programs. It provides workshops by leading jazz musicians such as the one in February of 1982 at which Jane performed and composed during a "Meet The Composer" concert. "To perpetuate the essence of jazz, it is important to educate the kids so someone will carry on," she explained. "There doesn't seem to be a group to replace those performing now. Our flagship in the New York state public schools will be followed by programs in Wisconsin and Florida."

Jane stated that in New York City, musicians are not paid as well as in other areas of the country. Many of her colleagues tour Europe and Japan where they receive good pay, but she isn't too keen on travel since she's been nearly everywhere she cares to go. Because of her long association with baseball, Jane has furnished organ music for baseball commercials. She also wrote the music and played the organ for a TV and radio commercial for Russ Togs. She is pleased that the Milt Hinton Trio has been so exceptionally well-received. Future dates on her schedule include several concerts in Florida, where she sometimes vacations. "Jazz is not for the faint of heart," Jane warns. "It is a battle of music and wits. If you really believe in your worth, as I do, then no sacrifice is too great or battle too rough. It's a siren song," she concluded. "Once you're in it, you can't quit. If you can quit, then you were never in it."

Molly MacMillan

Molly MacMillan of Scotia, New York, was a music major who now teaches and plays piano in an all-women group, Second Hand Rose. "I enjoy performing with other women musicians." she said. "But we definitely had some trouble with club owners who wouldn't take us seriously, and we worked for pennies at first." Listening to Sarah Vaughan was the impetus she needed to pursue a career in jazz. Then as a teenager in Schenectady, she met a jazz musician named Rio Clementi who took time to talk and listen to her. That reinforced her decision. "Because women paved the way before me, I have felt equally judged and accepted as a pianist," she said. "I think being a keyboardist helps in that respect. I want to be less concerned with being a woman and more concerned with being a warm musician." She admires the warmth and mastery of Marian McPartland and the ability of Joanne Brackeen to express so much of life right now through her music. She also has a high opinion of Bill Evans and Oscar Peterson.

"Learning what a racket the business world and recording industry can be was a disappointment," she said. "Adaptability is essential — handling the right role in the right job in the right place and staying sane!" To Molly, jazz seems as demanding a field technically and business wise as classical piano (she studied the classics for 13 years). "I prefer acoustical playing," she said, "and at times didn't think I'd ever be good enough. It was discouraging." When performing, she needs structure enough to lay a boundary, then can fly within, harmonically and rhythmically. "I think some people choose to stick with the past, and it's strong enough to survive. But jazz is a living art, and we should keep experimenting," she said. "Once during a gig in the Catskills, a sax player, drummer and I started 'Green Dolphin Street' as a whim," she said. "We took off *together*. It surprised us all. I want that spontaneous excitement!"

At one point in her life Molly was told she would never play again. Her right hand had been injured when shut in a car door. So she decided to take up the French horn and teach full time. but later she was able to return to the piano.

Young women need to be taught and encouraged, she feels. Her advice to a fledgling jazz pianist is, "Get out there and wail!"

Consuela Lee Moorehead

"I knew I *had* to play the music," Consuela said. "I had no choice." She was born in Tallahassee, Florida, but spent most of her childhood years in Snow Hill, Alabama. Both parents were musicians.

It was her mother, a "classical" pianist, who first taught her to play when she was four. Later Consuela was a music major in both college and graduate school.

"Though by the age of 17 my innate creative abilities were very apparent, I was not encouraged by the music department at Fisk University," she recalled. Her years of playing the classics taught her technique and control, but she also felt the training inhibited her total freedom necessary for improvisation. "The European concept of performance (for the performer and audience) is the exact antithesis of jazz or African-American music," she said. Alphonso Saville, a pianist from Little Rock, Arkansas, greatly influenced Consuela's decision to play jazz. "He treated the piano like an orchestra," she stated. "His voicings were impeccable, clean and crystal clear."

The woman musician she most admired was Mary Lou Williams, whom she met in New York when she was just starting out. "She encouraged and inspired me to move ahead in performance and writing," she remembered. "We were friends until her untimely death." The only women's group she remembered performing with was a band led by trumpet player Norma Carson in the early 1950's in New York. "I enjoyed it immensely," she said. But there were occasional episodes that were frightening to the young musician too. Years later, she can laugh about them. One occurred during the 1950's in a club outside Newark, New Jersey. "I was the only woman in the band," she said. "A woman came into the club looking for her man. When he ran into the men's room, she went berserk and started shooting a pistol. The bandleader said, 'Keep playing! Keep playing!' That was the first time I knew I could play the piano while my head and body were *under* the keyboard."

As a pianist with The New York Bass Violin Choir, she performed at prestigious New York concert halls, jazz festivals and college campuses across the country. She also worked with The Descendants of Mike and Phoebe and The Richard Davis Trio. She likes to communicate with her listeners. She shared a joyous moment which had recently occurred during a performance in Norfolk, Virginia. "I was play ing at a large Baptist church," she said. "The audience of about 2000 was totally involved in what I was playing. Their reaction was stunning." Musicians the world over strive for those moments when euphoria takes over during a performance. Consuela tried to verbalize her feelings when that happens. "I feel *centered*," she said. "Every note that's hit seems to be right. There is complete absorption in the music, and complete relaxation. So, complete enjoyment for me, and hopefully, the audience." She feels at her creative best when playing her own compositions and jazz classics such as Billy Strayhorn's "Lush Life."

The busy pianist admits to being a sports fanatic who loves college and pro basketball and football. Not satisfied to be an armchair athlete, she regularly exercises and eats sensibly to stay in shape. Following in the footsteps of her mentor Mary Lou Williams, she too is sharing her wealth of musical knowledge with the younger generation. In the summer of 1980, she returned to the place of her musical roots, Snow Hill, Alabama. There she founded the Spring Tree/Snow Hill Institute for the Performing Arts. She now spends part of her year there, teaching and passing on her musical concepts to others.

Nina Sheldon

Nina Sheldon has some advice for women considering a career as a jazz pianist. "Prepare yourself to be twice as good as almost all men. Expect to lead your own groups for the most part, and develop spiritual serenity, if possible." Nina Sheldon's credentials are impressive, so she must know what she's talking about. She received a full scholarship to Tanglewood, won second prize in the International Composers Competition, acquired a National Endowment Grant in 1978 and was appointed visiting lecturer in jazz history at Peabody Conservatory. She led the group Aerial (Carline Ray, bass; Barbara Merjan, drums; Barbara London, flute; and Jane Ira Bloom, saxophone) which performed at the Newport Jazz Festival, Lincoln Center, Dearborn Women's Jazz Festival, and won the combo contest at the 1979 Kansas City Women's Jazz Festival. Nina (with bassist Bob Bodley) later participated in the 1982 Kool Jazz Festival in Purchase, New York. "There seems to be an emotional closeness and empathy when performing with other women," she said. "Also, with good players, a lot of pride."

Nina had done extensive club work including stints at The Blue Note in Paris and New York's Sweet Basil, Jimmy Weston's, (where she followed Dorothy Donegan) and the Village Gate (where for three years she led a house trio which opened for Dizzy Gillespie, Charlie Mingus, Stan Getz and others). Her work in New York garnered good reviews in *The New Yorker*, *The New York Times* and *Down Beat*.

Nina has been called a human dynamo and her playing has been described by critics as bold, ferocious and wild during her more

Nina Sheldon.

energetic moments. Quiet ballads bring out her reflective nature as she vocalizes, often in Portuguese. She can warm up a reserved audience within minutes by making a few witty observations or singing satirical lyrics to an old standard like Charlie Parker's "Au Privave." She calls her version "Gynacology." She has run the emotional gamut from euphoria felt when walking onto the stage after Art Blakey performed, tapping into the energy still present, and playing her own music for 2,000 people, to a joyless month spent performing with "a sadistic, sexist, antisemitic drummer."

Nina admires Herbie Hancock's inventive integration of bebop and modality, Bill Evans' harmony, space, simplicity and feeling and the new ideas Chick Corea and McCoy Tyner brought to the art. Most of all, she likes Joanne Brackeen for her unique harmonic, rhythmic and melodic concepts that move and inspire her. "Joanne was a major influence on me," she said. "When I first heard her, it was like a poem speaking to a reader who has her idea expressed for her for the first time. It was hearing many of my conceptions in embryo." Besides the mutual support she shares with Joanne Brackeen and Jill McManus, Nina credits Sonny Stitt, George Coleman and Nick Brignola for hiring her; Reggie Moore and Jim McNeely for sharing new concepts; and her parents, teacher Richie Bierach, and Marian McPartland for support.

There have been discouragements along the way too. Nina was told by a record producer that no one wanted to record a female jazz player. She feels male musicians naturally lean towards getting together with their old pals, with whom they feel comfortable. "We grow through playing with better players and most of those are men, so it is important not to segregate ourselves," she said. "But we have a problem just being *thought* of to do certain gigs and play in jam sessions, both of which are *vital* for learning." Because of the increased number of talented young women who have entered an essentially male field, Nina thinks the situation will improve. "Male musicians and the public are a *little* more accustomed to the possibility of excellence in a female musician," she said. Her response to the timeworn comment, "you really play great, for a woman," can vary from, "You've got good ears,for a guy," to a patient explanation, depending on her mood.

Nina hopes her first record (with Dave Liebman, Eddie Gomez, Mike Di Pasqua and Lawrence Killian), released on the P.M. Records label the fall of 1982, will be followed by many more. She strives for excellence, an instantly recognizable style, a body of compositions uniquely her own, higher pay and a more widespread reputation. "I really love to play," she said. "It makes up for all the hardships. I support myself doing what I love, and that's very important." There was a time when Nina considered doing something else. "Very early on, I got so discouraged I went for one semester each, for *three* different masters' degrees!" she admitted. "But each time a good gig came along and I dropped out."

Lee Shaw

In 1957 Lee was not entirely fulfilled by her music. She had studied classical music from the age of five and continued, without interruption (even during the summers), until she had earned a master's degree. Becoming established as a classical accompanist, writing and selling material to singers and teaching were what she had worked so hard for, yet something was missing. Then she heard jazz and decided to pursue a career as a jazz pianist. While working as an intermission pianist at Mr. Kelly's in Chicago, she was able to hear Ella Fitzgerald, Billie Holiday and other jazz singers who appeared with their own trios. Friends Max and Jean Miller took her to hear Count Basie at the Blue Note. That experience enforced her desire to learn to play the wonderful music she heard. "I have never regretted it," she said, "although the cost of playing only the music I believed in has been very great and I had to adjust my style of living to the income of a dues-paying jazz musician."

The extensive training in the classics has served her well and she does occasionally teach and perform classical music. "It has given me more 'vocabulary' to use in improvisation, improves my ability to 'structure' a solo with balance, form and contrast ... to tell a story," she said. "I also feel it has been detrimental in a way. I am, to some extent, "programmed" so that I am not as exploratory as I might be."

Lee has always performed to good reviews, beginning in the 1960's when she appeared at the Village Vanguard, The Embers, Birdland and The Apartment, where she was held over. In 1963 she married drummer Stan Shaw who has played in their trio ever since. Lee credits him with tutoring her, acquainting her with the jazz idiom and taking care of the business and mechanics of performng. "I asked Oscar Peterson to take me as a student, and he did," she said. He shared with her his philosophy which affected her concept of the music. "It was one of the most rewarding experiences of my life." Bill Evans, Joanne Brackeen and Marian McPartland are a few of the pianists she admires, Marian especially for her tremendous involvement with promoting jazz on all levels.

Lee herself has conducted programs on the history of jazz piano, presented lecture recitals at grade schools and high schools, held clinics, and taught jazz improvisation courses in New York and Florida. During graduate studies in Puerto Rico, she took part in jazz workshops. The pianist once returned to Ada, Oklahoma, where she was raised, and dropped in at the East Central College campus where she performed unannounced for the music students and faculty. "Jazz is coming to be considered a staple in most schools on all levels," she said. "The young realize that jazz encompasses many styles, so there is much to choose from. The image of the jazz musician has improved greatly. I think the women's movement has helped, and women are able to move

Lee Shaw.

more easily into what traditionally was men's work." But Lee has en-
dured many disappointments and feels women embarking on a jazz
career should be aware of what they're getting into. Important are
timing (being in the right place at the right time), saying "yes" to every
possible opportunity (even if you have to find out HOW to do
whatever it is after you'd said "yes") and being lucky enough that your
talent and the demand for it occur simultaneously. "We had just begun

working at Birdland, great exposure, when it closed," she said. "We had been at The Embers in New York three times when it closed. Joe Franklin wanted us for the trio on his show if it became syndicated. We appeared on his show several times, then the syndication fell through. We played Harlem many times and would have gone back, but the riots occurred. Joe Glaser, head of Associated Booking Agency and mentor of Louis Armstrong and others, had just begun to take an interest in us, and he died. Columbia Records was interested but it was at a time during the 1960's when jazz was not selling so they didn't sign us ... and on and on and on."

Playing jazz well is still rewarding to Lee and playing every performance better than the last requires all the factors to be right: feeling good, warmed-up, good piano, good sound and allowing the piano to play itself. "That is the most effortless playing possible—the feeling that the piano is playing itself," she said. "The first time I really felt a "groove" (a rhythmic pulse so strong that it seems to take over the body and mind) was at a hotel in the Catskills with my husband and bassist Eddie Jones who had recently left the Basie Band. The older Basie bands achieved this frequently. All the players "feel" the time at exactly the same time and same way. We were playing for a typical Catskill weekend crowd, but they weren't dancing (to the alarm of the manager). We were quite willing to play music for them to dance to, but the music must have been communicating something else to them, so they behaved as though they were at a concert, just listening and applauding wildly after every tune. During that evening, we repeatedly hit a "groove." THAT must have been what the audience felt. My reaction was that of floating and feeling as though I was not even breathing. At the end of the set, the audience stood and applauded for a long time."

In 1980, after living in Florida for four years, the Shaws moved back to Albany and threw a party with the proceeds going to the American Cancer Society and the Capital District Jazz Society. Music from noon to midnight was provided by Lee, Stan, Nick Brignola, Emily Remler, Pepper Adams, Al Grey, Howard McGhee, George Coleman and other area musicians who played for more than 200 jazz fans. Since then Lee has worked steadily at jazz emporiums, concerts and festivals in the New York area. And the trio's first record is due to be released on Sound-Wise label.

Lee's playing is reminiscent of Debussy at times, and shaded by the influence of Oscar Peterson. While delivering tunes in the driving Basie style, her power seems incompatible with her small stature. "I sometimes must play hard because my temperament makes me do that," she said. "And I must have developed a lot of strength in my hands, arms and back, for my size."

Lee is known for giving credit to others, whether they share the bandstand with her or have put in a good word for her along the way, as Zoot Sims did when he recommended them for a gig at the Half Note. "So many musicians have helped me in so many ways that it is impossible to acknowledge them all. I just try to pass on to younger musicians what I have learned."

Noreen Grey

Noreen Grey was born into a jazz family. Both her parents are jazz musicians who traveled on the road before she was born. They continue to play, mostly within the Racine, Wisconsin, area where they live. Her younger brother is also a jazz musician. She "dabbled around at the piano" and learned to read a few notes while still very young. Then formal lessons began when she was seven. While in high school she made the decision to become a jazz musician. She was also considering veterinary school, but music won out. "I've never regretted my choice," the young pianist said, "though I do love my pets and feel animals are important."

Art Tatum, Mary Lou Williams, Erroll Garner, Joanne Brackeen, Tommy Flanagan, Thelonious Monk, and Marian McPartland are among the many pianists she likes to listen to. She feels that all forms of jazz should be appreciated, that all of it is meaningful. "If not for the older forms of jazz, the music wouldn't be where it is today," she said. "We must appreciate *every* step of its evolution and learn from that. Who knows where our experimentation will take us?"

When she was a student at the University of Wisconsin at Eau Claire, Noreen played with Clark Terry's All Girl-All Star Band at the 1976 Wichita Jazz Festival in Kansas. The girls were selected from colleges all over the country. Though a few musicians bickered over solos, for Noreen it was a positive experience. "We had few rehearsals before the concert, but the band came together well," she said. "Clark is a great guy. He was very encouraging and wonderful to work with."

Noreen moved east five years ago, despite being told of "cut-throat competition" and "getting lost in the shuffle." That didn't bother her: "Everyone has something different and special to offer the music world. That's what makes it so exciting—being a part of the whole thing."

Noreen Grey.

While conducting seminars at the University of Wisconsin, Joe Morello, a "drummer's drummer," had met Noreen and heard her play. Morello was drummer with the Dave Brubeck Quartet for eleven years. In 1978 when he formed a quintet, he hired Noreen as his pianist. They debuted at Hoppers in New York City where John S. Wilson of *The New York Times* heard her. He approved of the "enlivening, two-handed pianist who moves around the keyboard in an

imaginative fashion using phrasing that is provocatively rhythmic."
The newcomer received favorable comments in other newspaper
columns as well. Noreen played with Morello's group for nearly two
years. They appeared as a trio, quartet or quintet mostly through the
Eastern part of the country. The drummer sometimes introduced
young curly-haired Noreen as "Little Orphan Annie from Racine,
Wisconsin," and often expressed his pride in her.

In 1981 Noreen played with Howard McGhee at the Kool Jazz
Festival in New York City. "That was my first time playing at the
festival," she said. "It was a real high—my insides were jumping up
and down." Later that year she performed in a jazz faculty recital at the
University of Bridgeport in Connecticut where she teaches jazz piano
part-time. Noreen's trio, with Earl Sauls on bass and Ron Marbuto on
drums, played ten selections. The group had worked together before in
the New York-New Jersey area. A 1982 engagement with bassist Stephen Roane at Griff's Plaza Cafe in New York again caught the attention
of John S. Wilson. He approved of Noreen's solos which displayed
"appealing individuality, a blend of several pianistic sources ... that
show her moving in a direction that is her own."

She has found most male musicians to be very fair and accepting of her as a musician. Though others often assume she's the singer
of the group, after they hear her play, they usually are surprised and
complimentary. However once while working in a club, Noreen en-
dured a significant "disappointment in humanity." A musician whom
she was scheduled to work with later that week paid her a visit. "He
was vulgar and offensive, making blunt sexual remarks to me, the
waitresses and others," she said. "Even while my group was performing, he was loud and sarcastic. I ended up not doing the gig with him.
I didn't want to take the abuse." If a man really feels she's less of a
musician because she's a woman, Noreen says that's *his* problem. She
suggests that instead of worrying about the sex of a musician, he try
closing his eyes and listening to the music!

Besides performing, composing, and working on the jazz
faculty at the University of Bridgeport, Noreen teaches at jazz camps
and clinics. When performing, she hopes to express herself in a personal way and evoke an emotional response from an audience. After a
recent jazz concert, one of her young students approached her with a big
smile. The student patted her chest and said, "I felt it right here."
Noreen says, "That meant a lot to me."

Miranda Hentoff

"Jazz is learnable, not inborn," Miranda said. A recent graduate of Manhattan School of Music studying for her master's degree, Miranda Hentoff mostly does solo work in lounges in and around New York City. It was Bill Evans' artistry that influenced her to choose a jazz pianist's life. She finds his handling of the piano flawless. "His voicings are impeccable," she said. "His improvisations make sense."

Miranda didn't play the piano until she was 14 years old. She then began classical study which lasted 10 years. "Learning the classics helped me develop technique, musicality and good ears," she said. "If I can control five voices in a Bach fugue, I'll have an easier time controlling my own lines in improvisation."

For Miranda, creativity is the most important factor in her art. To search for *different* ways to express feelings is prime. "Experimentation is positive regardless of possible 'ugliness' along the way," she said. "Anyone can copy or work for technique, but creativity separates the artists from the mechanics."

Being a woman did not generate problems of equal pay or being accepted on an equal basis with men. She would tell a novice in the business to be assertive. She has found that a woman may have to prove herself a little more at first, but if she has ability, it will be recognized. "Maybe I did have to learn how to deal with men 'coming on' to me," she said, "but men have that too, though not as often or overtly as women." Miranda sees the future opening up for women musicians, with more and more female personnel in orchestras and big bands. She feels that good musicians will get the respect they deserve.

Her wish is to express herself with interest and uniqueness through her playing. She considers composition, both spontaneous or belabored, the ultimate musical joy: "To always create is a thrill a jazz musician has to enjoy at all times!"

Patti Bown

Patti Bown is a tall, handsome, affable woman whose piano playing can sweep the most sedate singer or group of musicians into a pounding swing. Her artistic talents are varied, though she concentrates on music. Erroll Garner and Arthur Rubenstein are her idols.

Patti Bown.

Patti's father was the son of a freed slave. Her mother's parents were a black woman and an Irishman. Orphaned at 12, her mother was sent to live with relatives. After she worked her way through school, she got a job as a beautician in Canada and returned to get her brother from an orphanage. Patti's parents met while in Canada, married and moved to Seattle where they raised eight children. "My father had an artistic temperament," Patti said. "He just could not work in the South where black people weren't supposed to think. He came North to work as a chef for the railroad." When his wife asked permission to buy something, he usually said no. A neighbor's sister had a piano for sale, and Mrs. Bown wanted that piano so badly she started praying to St. Jude. "I don't know if St. Jude had anything to do with it," Patti laughed, "but the woman died and our neighbor was left with all her furniture. My mother talked her into selling us that piano for ten dollars!"

Patti, her mother and sisters all played by ear. The family was delighted that Patti, a meddlesome toddler, finally found something to occupy her while her mother went about her work or fixed other women's hair. Bartering was common then and people often gave a dozen eggs, a chicken or whatever they happened to have in exchange for services. The three older sisters shared an hour piano lesson with Mrs. Simpkins, an elderly woman who was inclined to doze off while her students played. When Patti was six, she was allowed to take lessons too. By listening to her sisters, she played her way through the Thompson books by ear, earning a star on every page. "Then one day she just happened to turn to a strange page," Patti remembered. "When she realized I couldn't read the music, she told my mother I had been faking, and I got a beating." From then on, Mrs. Simpkins assigned unfamiliar and dissonant music, and the girl learned to read.

Patti played everything she heard on the radio too, and eventually the family got a record player. "We were always buying my mother gifts," she said. "$5 down and $99 to pay." The girls presented their mother with a record player and two records, "Slow Freight" by Glenn Miller and Billy Stayhorn's "Chelsea Bridge" by the Ellington band. Those were their only records for a long time, and Patti learned to play along with them on the piano. Blues songs she learned from her mother who, though raised a Catholic, sometimes went to the black church to enjoy the music. "Gospel singers visited the Church of God and Christ which was near our home," Patti recalled. "The music was like a magnet pulling my sister and me. We'd go there and beat on a dishpan in time with the music, knowing we'd later get punished for leaving our yard."

Patti stayed after school to take classical music lessons from a nun. Because she couldn't afford to buy the classical music she was learning at a rapid pace, she took home thick music books from the library. She also carried around an unabridged dictionary and a music dictionary which she pored over in her attempt to learn more. "That nun saw all the library books and what I was trying to do, so she kept me longer after school," Patti said. "She started teaching me harmony and solfege and that was the beginning of my learning what was inside the music." Already proficient in playing "serious" music, Patti found that when she was alone, she created her own music and found that more demanding than playing by a prescribed rule. Because her mother was interested in nurturing her daughters' creativity, Patti was exposed to many types of music. Mrs. Bown usually managed to scrape together enough money so her children could attend concerts by Rubenstein and other classical artists. Patti's sister Edith went on to play classical concerts both in the United States and Europe. "When my older sisters went to dances, my mother would tell my father to take me to the hall and park outside," she said. "My sisters inside would open a window so we could sit in the car and listen to the band."

Patti remembers her home as one filled with love and visitors of all types, from a ship's captain for Thanksgiving dinner to a circus giant who ate on the back porch. An old carpenter was called in periodically to fix the piano bench which broke from the constant use by the four girls. "Music was a catalyst," Patti said. "It brought such happy feelings to our home." The youngster played at black funerals, concerto contests and with visiting musicians. When she was ten, she inherited her sister's job playing for Saturday morning dance classes at Sevilla Fort's dance school. Later she had her own quintet which played at the Seattle Army Officers' Club on Sunday afternoons. Even though she was underage, she managed to get into black nightclubs to hear Quincy Jones and Ray Charles, other Seattle musicians, who also played tenor against Billy Tolles and Dexter Gordon in the "battle of the tenors." Patti gained experience from playing with them.

After graduating from high school at the age of 16, she attended Seattle University on a scholarship. Her mother wanted her to pursue a career as a concert pianist, but Patti knew she had to play jazz. "She died not really understanding why I had to do what I had to do," Patti said. "I got the feeling that after she died, maybe in the spirit world, she understood."

In 1956 she moved to New York City and started freelancing as an accompanist and band pianist. She had been warned it wouldn't be easy and it wasn't. Eventually she got work and became acquainted with the music scene. "I remember one time I had a gig up in the country with a band that was strung out on drugs," she said. "I was so square I didn't know what was happening, but wondered why they were all so tired." There were times when she had trouble getting paid for a gig because she hadn't been "friendly" when approached by the leader. Though she was young, she had to learn to be assertive in order to travel and work with other musicians without being taken advantage of.

Patti made her first record, "Patti Bown Plays Big Piano," in 1958. A man who had heard her play at Birdland called her the next day and took her to Nat Shapiro at Columbia Records. One of her tunes from that record, "G'won Train," became a theme for a matinee show on WNEW radio and was played by different bands. Even though several of her tunes were hits and are still on the air, Patti received little in the way of royalties, despite the help of lawyers. "That was my first encounter in dealing with big business," she said.

She was touring Europe with Quincy Jones' band when the record was released in 1959. From 1962 to 1964 she was musical director for Dinah Washington, traveled with Sarah Vaughan for a while and appeared at the annual Newport Jazz Festivals. "At the time, Dinah Washington was one of the world's greatest entertainers," she said. "But sometimes she was edgy and the slightest thing, maybe a request for a song, would become a racial issue with her. Seconds later, we'd be in the middle of a scene." Dinah bought Bob Cummings' old plane and traveled to jazz concerts and club engagements around the country. The plane was also used to fly her group to Mississippi to support Dr. Martin Luther King, Jr. "The plane had no pressure in the cabins," Patti said. "Once when we landed in Syracuse, everyone was on the floor but Dinah. She grabbed the microphone and was talking away, informing the tower that Dinah Washington was about to land. She had the energy of four people."

Patti can remember having to arrange for them to sleep in a private home in Tampa because of the lack of a decent black hotel. They appeared there at a dance for the NAACP with National Guardsmen surrounding the building.

She recalled being refused work in a network studio because a woman harpist had "recently messed up a modulation from a B-flat to an E-flat when she had her monthly." It didn't matter how well Patti could play. No more women were being hired.

"People were starting to call me for records," she said. "I got established doing all kinds of commercial records." Her recording work included sessions with Benny Carter, Nina Simone, Charles Mingus, Sonny Stitt, Duke Ellington, Aretha Franklin and others. Her first big band record date was with Quincy Jones. "Before the session began," Patti said, "one of the musicians said loudly, 'Oh, a bitch is gonna play the piano.' And all the fellas cracked up laughing. They laughed their insides out." Patti was hurt, but decided that the men were not accustomed to recording with women. "They seemed to feel that women were always trying to cop a plea," Patti said. "Women were known for being pretty, and playing lightly, and always having reasons why they couldn't complete something because they had problems with their bodies. So I just went ahead and played."

And she is still playing in her pulsating style, while she happily hums along. Besides studio work, she has appeared at concerts at Carnegie Hall and in Mexico City. Her pianistic talents were shared at jazz programs at Bennington College and Rutgers University. Marian McPartland interviewed her and played Ellington duets with her on radio. Patti joined Valerie Capers and Jill McManus to present Jazz Trilogy in 1980, prompting John S. Wilson to call her one of the most exciting performers in contemporary jazz.

The memorable performance of some of her compositions are

on videotape in the Library of Congress. She composed dance music for Joseph Papp's West Indian musical, "Tijean and His Brothers," and has had her music recorded by Count Basie, Quincy Jones and many other top musicians. "Dimity," a sensitive and loving tribute, was written in memory of her mother.

Patti has become involved more with television and the theatre, understudying two parts in "The Long Journey of Poppie Nongena," an off-Broadway play of 1982. She is currently working with poet/writer Japhet Okari, with whom she founded the Universal Arts and Folklore Organization. After receiving a grant from the National Endowment for the Arts in 1979, they did a show for the United Nations, the tape of which is still being shown. She also appeared at the "Smokin' Jam Session" at Lincoln Center during the 5th Annual Women's Jazz Festival in New York City. There are plans for a musical play for the African stage. Patti has already written some tunes in what she calls "Swahili Jazz," and she is intrigued by the possibility of someday writing an Irish-Jazz composition.

Patti feels threatened when people try to put her in a slot. She's often told when hired not to "go out" because the audience won't understand. "Others are telling me the limitations of my art, something I developed," she said. "I want to be free."

Isabelle Leymarie

Isabelle plays with various jazz and Latin jazz ensembles and has performed throughout the United States, Europe, Canada and Latin America. She recently appeared at Wings in New York City with bassist Todd Coolman. She feels her 10 years of classical training was a disadvantage; she would have preferred concentrating on jazz sooner.

Records of Mahalia Jackson and The Five Blind Boys primed Isabelle's interest in jazz. She also remembers seeing sheet music of Mary Lou Williams and "The Flat Foot Floogie" when she was very young. At 22 she made the decision to become a jazz pianist because of her love for the music, but was discouraged by her mother. "She told me it was a world of smoked-filled rooms, winos, and drug addicts," the musician recalled. "She said I'd have no stable income."

Isabelle thinks women should learn their skills well, and while talent and creativity are essential, a pianist has to work very hard to find her own style. Three musicians whom she considers great stylists are Kenny Kirkland, Mulgrew Miller and George Cables. "I also have the highest esteem for people like Kenny Barron, Frank Foster and Billy Taylor," she said. A long and steep road lies ahead for women musicians according to Isabelle, though the future of jazz looks good. She doesn't find that the women's rights issue has improved her lot much. "You just don't get as many jobs as your male peers," she said. "I've weathered a lot of racism, sexism, and competition. You can't really socialize with your fellow musicians. They tend to see you as a sexual object and their wives or girlfriends may feel threatened."

Isabelle has done many other types of work out of necessity. She is greatly interested in musicological research and is working on a book about Cuban music. But jazz is her first love. She sums it up. "Jazz is the most difficult musical form I know ... and the greatest."

Patti Wicks

"Jazz has given me the most fulfilling way of using my talent and creativity. I wouldn't trade my experience as a jazz musician for anything!" pianist Patti Wicks said recently. Though she studied classical music from the age of three until her graduation from State University College at Potsdam in New York, the petite musician didn't decide to become a jazz musician until her last year in college. "Up to that point, I was never sure what I would do with my music," she said. "I knew I didn't want a career as a concert artist and I wasn't interested in teaching." Two musicians who affected her decision were her piano teacher James Ball and Hal Miller, a drummer who shared his knowledge of jazz and his extensive record collection. "My classical training gave me a wide variety of musical ideas and interpretations with which to approach jazz improvisation," she said. "I know my playing is strongly influenced by impressionist works of Debussy and Ravel."

She moved to New York to begin her career and first worked with bassist Perry Lind, who taught her tunes she didn't know and introduced her to other good jazz musicians. She considered herself fortunate to play with Richard Davis, Frank Luther, Brian Torff and the late Sam Jones. "I can remember Sam Jones telling me, 'Patti, don't be afraid to call name musicians to work with you. Even call Ron Carter. If he's not tied up recording or on the road, he'll come out on a job with you.' That made me feel very good, because I had been hesitant about

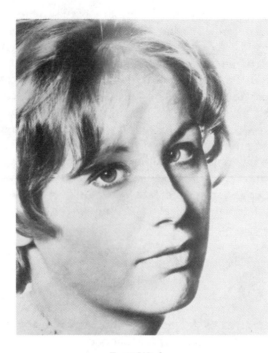

Patti Wicks.

calling Sam, who had such an illustrious career, recording with Oscar Peterson, Cannonball Adderly and a host of other jazz greats."

Patti's career took off in New York City, where she played in lounges, restaurants and jazz rooms. John S. Wilson of *The New York Times* found her music "full-bodied, vigorously rhythmic with a strong feeling for structure, dynamics and melodic essence." Columnist Muriel Montague wrote that Patti possessed a "sure voluptuous touch and her music comes out shimmering and sparkling and very often, quite stunning. She simply moves that piano any way she pleases." Her Manhattan engagements included The Half Note, Jimmy Weston's, Jilly's, West Boondock, The Apartment, Bradley's and Boomer's among others. She also made appearances on TV's "Jazz Adventures Show" and attracted a large following of college students. "I most enjoy playing ballads, such as Ellington's 'In a Sentimental Mood' and bossa novas," she said. "I tend to lean toward harmony (different interesting chord changes within a tune) and rhythm in my playing, rather than a fast technique in the right hand."

Patti's only experience with other women musicians was during a concert called "Women in Music" at Rutgers College. "The players were good and I found the experience delightful," she said. She admires Joanne Brackeen's strong modal style, Marian McPartland's control, and was very impressed with Jane Getz, a pianist no longer on the jazz scene.

Patti is still not satisfied with her playing and said she strives to consistently deliver that which she is capable of. "When I am playing my best, I feel exhilarated and wish it could go on forever," she said. "I feel good that my playing is under control and that I can express any idea I have." Patti occasionally vocalizes during a performance and remembers one evening when she wishes the audience hadn't been so quiet and attentive. It was during her rendition of "Small World, Isn't It?," a popular ballad. "One line had the words 'funny' and 'lucky' in it and I got the two words tangled up and you know what came out!" she said. "We all broke up. I still approach that particular phrase with a slight trepidation."

The future for women in jazz looks bright to Patti, who feels that girls exposed to jazz through school programs like Marian McPartland's will see the music as a respected art form and consider it as a career. The success of festivals such as the Kansas City Women's Jazz Festival is also encouraging to her. "It's important to keep jazz of the past alive so that young players coming up are aware of the various styles and are able to play them," she said, "and aren't just jumping on the bandwagon of experimental jazz without really knowing what they're doing." Patti feels a woman must be willing to dedicate herself to the music and not get sidetracked. She advises studying and playing with the best, if possible. "The late Sam Jones once advised me to always play with good musicians," she recalled. "They don't have to be name artists, just good players," he said. "Otherwise do a single."

Patti's recent engagements have been at various seaside resorts in Florida. Besides performing and composing, she practices by playing along with her favorite records. Playing pool and reading are relaxing to her. and she *loves* to dance. "I'd never consider giving up playing jazz," she said, "but just once I'd love to perform a dance act, a la Ann-Margret before I get too old!"

Ann Johns Ruckert

Ann was attending grade school and studying classical music. She enjoyed her piano lessons, but felt something was missing. Then one day she heard a tune on the radio by Count Basie. "That changed my life then and there," she said. "It was like coming home." The recording was Basie's "Queer Street," with a trumpet solo by Harry "Sweets" Edison. The girl was fascinated by the accent on the second and fourth beat instead of the first and third as in her pieces by Bach. "It gave a new feeling to the quarter note," Ann said. "At first the attraction was not the improvisation but the time feel."

Ann's grandfather had given her informal instructions before she started her piano lessons at the age of six. She acquired a deep understanding of the roots and science of the music from her classical training. At 16 she made a full commitment to music. "I have never been sorry," she said. "I feel I was born a musician, so it has been easier for me than some of my friends and family who had to agonize over what to do with their lives and what career to choose. For me it was just a matter of learning the discipline necessary for such a demanding profession."

Ann feels discouragement from others has been a continuing factor in her need for unwavering discipline. One of her teachers once told her the best she'd ever do was teach. As a timid 17-year old, she auditioned for a piano chair, and had to wait four hours while every male instrumentalist was tried. When she finally was on her way to the piano, a vocal chart was handed to her. "I was too shy to say anything, so I sang," she said, "and I got the job." From then on, she was a pianist-singer, which until recently she deeply resented. But an arthritic condition affected her playing. "I am deeply disappointed that my illness had taken a certain kind of technique from me," Ann said, "but I'm grateful that it has been replaced by a more advanced harmonic sense that gives me new pleasure and enables me to make a living as a studio singer."

Ann admires "Jane Jarvis and Joanne Brackeen not only for their music but because they never would sing, or play a gig that was not to their liking."

Ann said the pressure of not having equal rights, pay or respect from the male instrumentalists was too much for her. "My first husband, who is a jazz musician, sold my piano in the first years of our marriage," she said. "He felt it was too big for our pad." Ann also considers sexual harassment a professional hazard, especially when trying to get home safely after working until 2 a.m. "Men in the streets seem to feel any woman out at that hour must be a hooker or fair game," she said, "so after working five sets a night, one has to fight her way home, without even thinking of getting something to eat." However Johnny Richards and George Coleman have been a source of reassurance to

Ann, who said her two friends consistently support women instrumentalists who often are treated as an oddity when playing together. "You never hear of an all-male orchestra," she said. Ann gets encouraged every time she is hired for a job and feels she has been luckier than most. She said musicians in general are not as open and generous with each other as they could be. Jealousy is sometimes present. "But I find if you declare yourself to be friendly and helpful, that is usually the way you are treated in return," she said.

For listening pleasure, Ann prefers the keyboard proficiency of Jane Jarvis, Art Tatum, Joanne Brackeen, Red Garland and Harold Mabern, all for the same reason. "One note and I can tell who it is — they have a touch that is totally dissimilar but easy to identify."

In Anne's opinion, a bright future for women and jazz is inevitable because of the great music of the past that is there to build on. She says a woman considering a jazz career should "go for it," by coming to New York City and networking, once she has made a reputation in her hometown. "Don't wait to be discovered," she said, "and call me if you need the names of some good bass players."

Ann recently shared her musical expertise at workshops at the Jazz Gallery in New York City. Despite the dark rumors about jazz that she has heard for years, Ann is convinced that jazz is here to stay as well as the women who perform it. "We musicians don't have a choice," she said. "It's a calling we answer. That's all."

Corky Hale

It was the first day at music camp and a group of students were getting acquainted. Much to her distress, nine-year-old Merrilyn Hecht discovered she was not only the youngest, but the only girl without a nickname. The roster didn't include anyone named Corky, so that's what her new friends decided to call her. Today, after a notable career in jazz, the multi-talented musician still answers to that moniker.

Corky was born in Freeport, Illinois, and began studying classical music while still a toddler. She was accepted at the Chicago Conservatory when she was seven. Later she studied at Stevens College in Columbia, Missouri, and at the University of Wisconsin. "Then I went right to Hollywood," she said. "Back in the 1950's, that was a glamorous place to be." Though her parents tried to dissuade her from going, they reluctantly conceded and enrolled her at UCLA. "I never

Corky Hale and co-performer.

went to a single class," she recalled. "The first week I was there, someone heard me play, and I was hired to play piano and harp with the house band at the Coconut Grove."

Within a short time, she made her debut on television. She was invited to play piano and harp with Freddie Martin's rhythm section (bassist Lloyd Pratt and guitarist Al Viola). The two men had also played for Andre Previn whom Corky would work with later on in Los Angeles. They took her around Hollywood and introduced her to many people. It wasn't long before her career really took off. "A man called up and said, 'My name is George Liberace and my brother is a piano player. We're starting a new television show. We've heard you play and we want you for our show.' " The 19-year-old was to spend the next three years playing harp on the Liberace Show 52 weeks a year. She toured 44 states and also appeared in the movie, "Sincerely Yours," with his group. "I was very lucky!" she said. "I play the harp like a piano and that was in my favor." After that, she was hired for the Red Skelton Show, where Peggy Lee saw her and decided to hire her. Then followed piano work with the big bands of Ray Anthony, Harry James and Clark Terry. She was nearly always the only woman in the band. "The 1950's were marvelous," she said. "Both the music and my experiences were terrific." During the late 1950's she became Mel Torme's pianist and along the way teamed up with Billie Holiday for two months in Las Vegas and Los Angeles. That experience left a lasting impression on Corky. "She was wonderful to me," Corky said. "You rarely have a chance to work with such a legendary talent."

After a divorce in 1961, she moved to Italy where she lived for three years. She appeared weekly on a Rome television show, "Tempo on Jazz." In the summer of 1966 in London, she ran into Tony Martin, who asked her what she was doing in Europe. I don't know," she remembered saying. "I'm just drifting around." He invited her to return to the states as his piano player and she accepted. Club dates followed in Los Angeles, Fort Lauderdale and New York, where she settled in the fall of 1966. Then she met Mike Stoller of the songwriting team, Lieber and Stoller. "The most fantastic man in the world," Corky said of Stoller, now her husband. "When we met, we were in totally different musical bags. My friends were impressed. 'Oh, Mike Stoller wrote "Jailhouse Rock."' I'd say, 'What's that? I never heard of that.'"

The attractive musician recorded with Tony Bennett, Nina Simone, Gerry Mulligan and James Brown. In 1979, after not touring for several years, she joined a three-month, 29-city tour with Judy Collins. She played electric piano and sang backup. "I felt like Grandma," she said. "All the guys in the band were wonderful, but they were in their '20's." Corky found traveling by van from date to date quite different from the earlier days of touring with Liberace and others. "We were treated like royalty in those days," she said. We stayed in nice hotel suites and enjoyed champagne parties. I realized times had changed."

The diversely talented musician (she plays harp and flute, as well as sings, but regards the piano as her main instrument) has worked professionally since she was 17 and doesn't feel being a woman has held her back. "I don't like being categorized," she said. "Either you're a good player or you're not."

The 1980's presented more studio sessions and work at the Knickerbocker Saloon in New York's Greenwich Village, the Women's Jazz Festival in Kansas City, a six-night stint in Frankfort, Germany, and one at Maunkberry's in London, England. Studio musicians, Corky explained, tend to remain in the shadows. Though studio assignments provide enjoyable work, sometimes an artist needs individual recognition. Mike is supportive of Corky and urges her to get back in the limelight. Critics and fans alike are complimentary when she does. When appearing at Maunkberry's, her keyboard expertise was lauded in the London *Sunday Times* and Britain's *Stage and Television Today*. Critic Peter Hepple wrote, "...no feminine delicacy here, but a hard gutsy approach which brings smiles of approval to the faces of her British rhythm men...."

Over the years, the versatile musician has pursued various business interests. She owned a clothing store in Hollywood for 17 years and a restaurant called "Corky's" in New York during the 1970's. Her future plans include producing a movie filmed in Germany and Israel. However, a fulfilling domestic life takes precedence in Corky's busy schedule, and she doesn't intend to neglect her culinary talents. "I love to cook," she said. "I remember coming home at 2 a.m. from a job with the Harry James band. There'd be maybe 16 guys with their wives, and I'd cook for us all. "I'm very square. I've been all over the world, but I'm probably the squarest musician there ever was!"

Jill McManus

The first job Jill McManus had as a musician was working for an ill-tempered bar owner from 7 p.m. to 2 a.m., five nights a week. "I played in a trio," she said. "Horn players and singers sat in and asked for all the tunes I'd never heard of, in all the keys I'd never played in. I made fifteen dollars and used it to take a cab home." During this same period she was working days as a reporter-researcher at *Time*, where she wrote jazz articles and record reviews. Over a period of five years, she made the transition to become a professional jazz pianist. "I was a passionate late bloomer," she said. "Now that I see how difficult and absorbing the music is, I'm glad I finished college, had a good job, and traveled, so I have a bit of perspective on the world." She learned to joke about setbacks like trying to work a club with no piano or the three gigs that came in for the same night after a jobless month. As she said, "It's funny when two duos sit and stare each other down because the owner has booked you both by mistake."

During the past 10 years, Jill has become a competent pianist, composer and leader. She led the Jazz Sisters from 1975 to 1977 and played in quartets at New York's Salute to Women in Jazz in 1978, 1979 and 1980. She also assembled and led the All-Star Band at the Kansas City Women's Jazz Festival in March of 1980, and later that year she performed in a jazz trilogy concert with Patti Bown and Valerie Capers. Since 1977 she has played in duos, trios and quartets at clubs in New York, as well as in Europe and in the Caribbean.

Jill McManus.

Her driving style prompted columnist John S. Wilson to comment favorably on her "provocative lively manner." She's been described as romantic, tough and intriguing. Her playing reflects touches of Bill Evans, whose music, along with that of Bud Powell, was a major influence on her decision to change careers, and Roland Hanna, with whom she studied. "I admire Roland Hanna's immaculate construction, resolutions and classical fusion," she said. "He has been an inspiration to me and helped me get started with my own teaching."

Jill feels the different styles of jazz up to the present should be treasured and preserved without setting up limitations. "Jazz itself is creative," she said. "I think it's moving into a time of 'world music.' The people with the most talent and drive will succeed, but for those without 'world category' qualifications, it will be difficult."

Jill advises women who want a career as a jazz pianist to be totally determined to proceed at all costs — emotional, financial and physical. She also recommends having a second job. "It is slightly more rigorous than the priesthood, but more varied," she said.

The Jazz Sisters first played together in 1974 at the annual "Ladies' Day" at the New York Jazz Museum (now closed) when six women were randomly chosen. They warmed up and began playing. The interaction was so enjoyable they decided to meet again. Trombonist Janice Robinson was the only full-time musician. Bassist Lynn Milano, trumpet player Jean Davis, drummer Paula Hampton, tenor sax player Willene Barton and Jill all had other jobs. "We were actually treated as a novelty," she said, "but we were good enough to play some good jobs — opposite Mingus at the Village Gate, Town Hall, colleges and clubs. It was hard to find subs of our level, and our pay was cut if we had to use a male sub!" The Jazz Sisters found their audiences were appreciative of their music, while club owners and agents usually thought the performance needed choreography or suggested tight low-cut dresses.

Jill assembled and led the All-Star Band at the 1980 Kansas City Women's Jazz Festival. Playing Jill's compositions were Stacy Rowles (trumpet and flugelhorn), Jane Fair (reeds), Louise Davis (electric bass), Barbara Merjan (drums) and Janet Lawson (vocals). The combination of a compatible quintet and original material resulted in a superior performance before a huge crowd.

Jill's first album, *As One*, was recorded while in performance at the Fuge on New York's lower East Side. She and bassist Richard Davis, recording in relaxed surroundings, perfectly complemented each other on the five selections. Some of Jill's compositions have been recorded by other artists. Her work with duos and trios brought her together with musicians such as Pepper Adams and Sam Jones, for whom Jill wrote a touching poem in memoriam. "Bass players Brian Torff, Wayne Dockery, and Marc Johnson helped me get it together," Jill said. "And a very good sax player named Mike Citron."

Between her club engagements at Hanratty's, Bechet's, and Garvin's, she finds time to walk a few miles every week regardless of the weather, listen to music around the city, write poetry and meditate. "I read," she said. "Read about the tribulations of jazz musicians and about people who have persisted until they realized their ambitions. While working with jazz greats and leading the All-Star Band in Kansas City were heady experiences, Jill admitted the "best moments" had come on good playing nights while doing small gigs. "Only the band knew "It" was happening," she said. "I felt euphoric!"

Valerie Capers

Valerie Capers is a pianist-composer who leads a full jazz musician's life in New York City where she was born. Besides filling concert dates and cafe bookings, the blind musician shares her time and talent to help others. She was chosen to serve on the President's Committee for the Disabled in 1981, the Year of the Disabled. Valerie has been blind since the age of six, when an illness deprived her of her sight. Her early schooling took place at the New York Institute for the Education of the Blind. She then continued to study and obtained her bachelor's and master's degrees from the Juilliard School of Music.

A musical family initiated her interest in jazz. Valerie's brother Bobby worked with the Mongo Santamaria Band, playing flute and tenor sax. Her father was associated with Fats Waller, whose musical nuances have been noted in Valerie's playing. She formed her own trio and debuted as a recording artist on the Atlantic label.

Town Hall was the setting in January of 1977 for a concert featuring women jazz instrumentalists. Sharing the program with Valerie was friend Jill McManus, who led the Jazz Sisters, and Donna Summer's Peace Makers. Robert Palmer of *The New York Times* declared Valerie's performance "the highlight of the evening" and wrote that "the bristling density of Miss Caper's chordal passages and her habit of materializing melody lines out of lush tremolos are notably original." He praised her ballad playing for its "control of dynamics and depth of feeling."

A similar concert, "Jazz Trilogy," took place in 1980 at the Symphony Space Theatre on Broadway. The Valerie Capers Trio appeared with Jill McManus and Patti Bown, who both led their own trios during the performance. John S. Wilson of *The New York Times* wrote in his review that Valerie's playing rose to "driving, flamboyant passages that exploded with energy."

During 1981 the pianist appeared with Dizzy Gillespie in Redondo Beach, California, for "Concerts By the Sea," which were video-taped for a "Jazz America" television series. Her trio also performed at the 1981 Kool Jazz Festival and in concert at Alice Tully Hall, Lincoln Center. The following year she was one of the jazz artists chosen to participate in Summerpier, a series of free concerts in the port district among the historic sailing vessels and century-old buildings. Club work around Manhattan included Bradley's, Stilwende and Griff's Plaza Cafe, where a return engagement was arranged.

Valerie composes and conducts special jazz material which has

Valerie Capers. (Courtesy Louis Braille Foundation.)

been acclaimed by critics as outstanding jazz writing. In 1980 at the Avery Fisher Hall in New York City, her "150th Psalm" premiered. "Sing About Love," her jazz cantata involving the talents of 40 instrumentalists and vocalists, was conducted by Valerie at Carnegie Hall where it was first presented. Her jazz opratoria, "Sojourner," premiered at St. Peter's Church in New York in February, 1981. Valerie received a National Endowment for the Arts Award and the jazz work was presented in association with National Black History Month. In spite of a physical impairment, Valerie Capers has sustained and refined her musical aptitude to become an outstanding musician. Her talents as a performer, composer and conductor have earned her the respect of other musicians, both women and men.

Carla Bley

Carla Bley is a pianist/composer who expresses herself through her compositions and arrangements. The musician, whose face is barely visible behind her large eyeglasses and encompassing hair style, is considered to be one of today's most innovative jazz composers. Performances by the Carla Bley Band are never dull. Concert goers are treated to humorous and outrageous moments along with unique and stirring music. Even so, recent performances are considerably calmer than the earlier days when gags abounded and the musicians wore bald wigs. Now they are content to simply play their music and occasionally boo the audience to liven things up.

Carla, whose father was a piano teacher, was born in Oakland, California. She studied piano and sang as a child, then married musician Paul Bley in 1957. She started writing for him and others including Steve Kuhn, Gary Burton, Art Farmer and Don Ellis. In 1964 she was one of the charter members of the Jazz Composers Guild which was founded to help jazz musician/composers. That organization was short-lived, but paved the way for The Jazz Composers' Orchestra Association (JCOA) created by Carla and Austrian trumpeter Michael Mantler in 1966. The primary purpose of the JCOA was to provide support for composers creating expansive works for jazz orchestras. Funded by the state of New York and private sources, the organization was able to conduct workshops and present concerts. Recordings were also released on JCOA's own label.

Carla divorced Paul and married Michael Mantler, with whom she still works. In 1972 they founded the New Music Distribution Service which provides an outlet for recordings on small independent labels. The not-for-profit organization sends out free catalogs describing more than 2,000 esoteric recordings, ranging from chamber music to New Music. About half are jazz recordings. Record sales support the service along with contributions from national, state and private foundations.

Carla has performed and worked on radio and television in Holland, Germany and Italy. She has lectured, scored films and participated in sessions at the Creative Music Studio in Woodstock, New York. She started her own record company, WATT, with Michael Mantler and performs with her band at concerts. *Live* (ECM W-12) was recorded at San Francisco's Great American Music Hall with her 10-piece ensemble, and released in the summer of 1982. On a recent television show, "Women in Jazz: The Creative Force," Carla talked about her band and the music she composes for it. "If you have your own band, you can hear what you wrote the next day," she said.

Since other bands never play her compositions exactly to her liking, Carla prefers to see that the music is executed precisely as she intends. In exchange for total control of the form, the composer and leader delegates solo space to the band. She admitted to being spoiled in having complete authority. "And I don't want to lose it," she concluded.

Sharon Freeman

Sharon Freeman left home to follow the beat of jazz. The attractive young black woman recently appeared on "Women In Jazz — Breaking Through," a television series moderated by Marian McPartland. Her parents expected her to acquire a bachelor's or master's degree in music in order to teach. "Because you need security," Sharon said. "After you do all of these things, you get married. A lot of people find it very difficult to break out of that mold. But I did." She put herself through school while working and teaching. The first important job that came along was playing French horn, now a familiar instrument in jazz groups. That led to work as pianist, arranger and composer. She has gained further recognition from performing at festivals featuring fine women instrumentalists. In 1982 she and other notable jazz artists appeared at the five-day Wolf Trap Jazz Festival in Virginia.

For Sharon and other women jazz instrumentalists, an important breakthrough came with the establishment of festivals dedicated entirely to them, places where they could play and gain exposure and recognition.

Judy Carmichael

In late 1982, a dynamic self-taught stride pianist made her New York debut and shocked everyone who heard her. Instead of the usual wide-shouldered male ragtime performer, the musician turned out to be a slim blond woman in her twenties.

"Where does the power come from," she was asked, "and why are you playing this music?"

"Because I like it," she replied.

Judy grew up in California and wasn't very interested in her piano lessons. Her grandfather offered $50 to any grandchild who could play "Maple Leaf Rag." Judy taught herself the piece, collected the reward, and never took another lesson.

Her love affair with rag continued as she added more tunes to her repertoire. While attending California State College, she got a job replacing a regular pianist on his night off.

Hearing her first Fats Waller album when she was 21 led Judy to immerse herself in period recordings from the 1920's. She soon had as much work as she could handle and in 1977, was hired to play at Disneyland. Jackie Coon, a studio musician also employed there, heard and encouraged her.

Judy first visited New York in 1979. Even though her recording date fell through, she was invited to sit in with Roy Eldridge and Tommy Flanagan. She returned to her Disneyland job in California to play seven hours nightly during the week and at clubs on weekends.

When her first record, *Two Handed Stride* (Progressive) came out late in 1982, she accepted a two-week gig at Hanratty's in New York. Her debut brought amazement and praise from veteran musicians and critics alike. She brilliantly maneuvered her way through "Honeysuckle Rose," "Viper's Drag" and "Russian Rag" as well as piano novelty tunes from the 20's like "Dizzy Fingers."

Judy Carmichael is a refreshing enigma. How many young white female pianists have the natural ability to play in the style of legendary black men of nearly six decades ago? And where does she get the stamina to execute her hard-driving ragtime and stride piano?

Barbara London

Barbara is a pianist-flutist-singer who equally divides the attention and expression she channels through each of her three instruments. She is also a poet, composer and lyricist. Disappointments have been frequent during her career, especially serious health problems which resulted in long periods away from her music. In the interim, she suffered a great deal of anxiety and depression, but became more philosophical in her outlook. She also started writing poetry on one such forced vacation, adding yet another creative outlet to her life. "I've learned over the years not to focus on the disappointments," she said, but rather to move forward and let go of the frustration as easily as possible. It's a challenge!" The attractive, dark-haired musician has considered other lines of work in addition to music, for example, working in the medical or health field, nutrition or counseling.

Her development as a jazz pianist evolved over a considerable period of time. She already played classical piano (having started studying at the age of six) when she was improvising on the flute. "I gradually started to improvise more on piano, looking for new harmonies," she said, "and often there were more jobs available on piano." Inspiration came from Joanne Brackeen, Bill Evans and Marian McPartland who first heard Barbara with the women's jazz group Aerial at the 1979 Kansas City Women's Jazz Festival. Aerial won the combo contest that year. "We met and spoke with her there and at other jazz events in New York City," she recalled. "She was complimentary and supportive. A friendship grew. I was able to call her for specific information about recording and gigs. She gave us job leads that she heard about. She even invited me to sit in with her in a club in Manhattan and another in Chicago!"

Barbara grew up in a musical family in northern Maine, and graduated summa cum laude from the University of New Hampshire. From 1972 to 1976 she traveled, performed and recorded with the group Morning Sky. From that time on, she had performed solo, with Aerial or with her own group. Her sparkling flute playing earned her critical praise in *Down Beat* and *The New York Times*. As a faculty clinician at several universities, schools and summer music camps, her teaching has focused on jazz improvisation and composition.

As a composer, Barbara draws on her background. "Alta's Song" was written two days before the death of her grandmother. "New Blues" combines a traditional blues form, a bebop line, and lyrics derived from an ongoing conversation with her father about music as a career. He was apprehensive about the environment and lack of security his daughter would be subjected to. "Superfluity" has been performed by a big band and celebrates nature, which Barbara deeply cares about. Though some of her pieces are totally notated, many are combinations of written and improvised sections. Her poetic talents have enabled her to write lyrics, adding another dimension to compositions.

Along with her own original music, her programs usually include jazz standards such as those of Duke Ellington, whose contribution to American music Barbara feels has only begun to be

Barbara London.

appreciated. "My musical influences are as varied as Bach, Chopin, the Beatles, family members, Roland Kirk, Bill Evans and Ed Corey, Rob Hope and other friends," Barbara declared. "Depending on my mood, I can enjoy a string orchestra, solo guitar, a cooking jazz quartet or informal banjo picking." The pianist constantly attempts to achieve a clarity of expression, variety of sounds and textures and a wide dynamic range. "But most importantly, I strive for a particular spirit to come through my music, a spirit which is hard to define," she said. "It embodies my beliefs and life experience." Music must be integrated into the lives of musicians, Barbara believes, and she especially emphasizes the importance of health in the total sense: physical, mental, emotional and spiritual. "Each of us must find and fulfill our own needs in terms of diet, exercise, environment, friends, vision and confidence," she said.

Unforgettable incidents dot Barbara's career, such as the performances in Kansas City and Newport and her grant-supported concert in New York City. "Those were 'glamorous' moments," she said, "but many bright moments, though probably insignificant to others, have occurred all along the way. The first time I played a duo with an old friend at a small New England bar after a long illness and absence, I was so high, I couldn't sleep for two days."

Barbara has very positive feelings about working with other women jazz artists, though she admits she was intimidated at the thought of seeking out other women at first. "I remember my trip into New York for Cobi Narita's first Salute to Women," she said. "I was unsure of how I would feel ... maybe uncomfortable or competitive in a negative way. But I was pulled into the energy and supportive network." According to Barbara, the general climate for women musicians has become more positive during the past five years, with the special women's programs being supported by both men and women. "More and more players are studying from the bottom up *and* forward," Barbara observed. "They are learning about the evolution of jazz in addition to experimentation. Their future is wide open and exciting."

Her problems have not been with male musicians so much as with men in management and recording positions. "There was often an attitude of condescension or a feeling from them that I wasn't legitimate, not seasoned enough," she said. "Some of this may have come from my own feelings of vulnerability and insecurity. I've worked hard to overcome those feelings and to assume a professional stance."

The musician, who has appeared at Lincoln Center, Avery Fischer Hall and the United Nations, stated that few jazz musicians make even an average income. So in order to achieve happiness in the profession, one must balance the hard work, discipline and methodical organization with the process of developing and with the joy and satisfaction one gets from playing. "Acceptance of one's limitations is as necessary as the motivation to push ahead as far as one's capabilities and unique abilities will allow," she said. "Defining one's *own* goals and taking a realistic look at what is required to meet the challenge is important, and a process in and of itself. Whether singing, playing the flute or performing at the piano, Barbara draws from both the discipline of her classical study and the autonomy of jazz experience. "I want to take listeners to new places, to see new designs, and hear new sounds," she concluded.

Marge Hilton

"I'm a great-grandma who plays jazz piano," the friendly musician said. "I thank God every day for the wonderful gift he gave me, my music." Marge raised four children while playing cocktail hours and night time jobs until 4 a.m. Looking back, she doesn't know how she did it, but said her love for her children and her music carried her through.

"I was an only child," she said, "and I loved music from the beginning. It was my brothers and sisters, since I was alone so much." Piano training began at the age of five and continued all through school. Though she also studied the violin and played in a string quartet and symphony, Marge always preferred jazz piano. Because the girl could play by ear any tune she heard, her teachers never demonstrated how a piece should be played, thus forcing her to learn the technical way. The pianist later was grateful for the technical knowledge she possessed. When faced with raising four children, she turned to her music as a means of support. "It just happened," she recalled, "I don't think I realized what I was doing." Marge played her first job in Erie, Pennsylvania, with a guitar player and a bass man. The money was used to buy groceries. She took all the work she could get, gaining assurance as time went on. "Joe Mooney was my greatest influence and very good friend," she said. "He showed me so much about chord progressions and also gave me a lot of confidence in doing what I felt. His playing is so sensitive."

Though Marge regrets that she has never had the opportunity to record, there have been extremely satisfying incidents during her career. Shortly after becoming a professional jazz pianist, Marge was invited to sit in with Count Basie and his band in Youngstown, Ohio. The musician never felt discrimination because of her sex, but was considered just "one of the guys."

At the urging of a friend who had moved to Florida, Marge went down in 1951 to look for work. She landed a job in Fort Lauderdale the first day she tried! Her children joined her and Marge began playing engagements from Miami Beach to Pompano. In 1960 she married businessman Harry Burt who loved music and took up the drums. "He was a natural," she said. Marge in turn learned to play golf, his favorite sport. A few years later, the couple formed their own jazz group which played at country clubs, weddings and private parties. "We traveled a lot," Marge said, "and always had our golf clubs and drums with us. We knew all the jazz musicians in the area. Every Memorial Day weekend, we had a "Harry Burt Day" to celebrate Harry's birthday. About 50 musicians and their wives came at noon and stayed for hours."

Marge became a widow in late 1981 and turned to her music for solace. She spent the following summer playing for dinner guests at her son's old English Inn near Estes Park, Colorado. Living in a studio near

Marge Hilton.

the Inn, she enjoyed the beauty of her mountainous surroundings and baked Florida Key Lime pies with the dozens of Key limes she had brought from home. The special dessert (priced at three dollars a slice) was so popular with the customers at the Inn, she baked over twenty pies!

Back home in Florida, Marge plays golf, swims and never plans to quit playing the piano. She tells young women that their future looks promising. "Since women's iib, anything can happen," she insisted. "You have to listen a lot and get as much experience playing with others as you can. I've had fun on the few occasions I've played with other women. I've never regretted being a jazz pianist and when I'm playing well, I just don't want to stop."

Shirley Horn

Shirley Horn was born in Washington, D.C., in 1934, and studied at Howard University Junior School of Music. When she was 17, she was playing classical music in a Washington restaurant, after which she gradually began singing and playing more in the jazz vein. She formed her own group to work in lounges and became more knowledgable about the innovative music that she favored over the classics.

Her 1959 album, "Embers and Ashes," brought her to the attention of celebrated musician Miles Davis who insisted Shirley's group come to New York and share billing with him at the Village Vanguard. From that prestigious engagement came a five-year-contract with Mercury Records. During the 1960's, she went to Hollywood to sing the theme songs in two of Sidney Poitier's films, "For the Love of Ivy" and "Dandy in Aspic." She also did work for television commercials and appeared at concerts in the New York and Washington areas. National Public Radio continues to rebroadcast her performances on "Jazz Alive."

Shirley took a self-imposed hiatus from performing in the late 1960's in order to focus more time on her family life. The gifted pianist with gentle, gossamer voice resumed her place in the limelight in the 1980's with a standing ovation at the Northsea Jazz Festival at The Hague, an appearance at the National Press Club, a concert date at the Corcoran Gallery in Washington and an engagement at Michael's Pub in New York City. "All Night Long," with Charles Ables and Billy Hart, was recorded live at the 1981 Northsea Jazz Festival. In June of 1982, Shirley's trio played at St. Peter's Church in New York City during the Universal Jazz Coalition 5th Annual Women's Jazz Festival. Charlie's was one of many clubs on her agenda that summer.

Others

Pianists Bertha Hope has had extensive professional experience on the music scene in New York City, including work with the Jimmy Castor Blues Band and Evelyn Blakey and Celebration. Bertha was featured with Blakey's group at "Big Apple Women in Jazz" showcase during the 2nd Annual Women's Jazz Festival in 1979. She is founder of Inner Spirit/Doug Hawthorne as well as a composer-arranger, who occasionally vocalizes. During the 1981 New York Kool Jazz Festival, she participated in the program, "Women Blow Their Own Horns." Bertha played with saxophonist Willene Barton's group, a swinging quartet which delivered up-beat tunes and ballads to good reviews.

Jessica Jennifer Williams is a contemporary pianist who has recorded group albums, one of which, "Orgonomic Music," was released in 1981. On that recording she abandoned electronic keyboards and returned to acoustic piano. Her playing has been compared to McCoy Tyner's.

Amina Claudine Myers was born in Arkansas in 1942 and as a teenager accompanied her school choir. After receiving a degree in music education, she taught school in Chicago for several years. In the 1960's she became affiliated with the Association for the Advancement of Creative Musicians and performed at the Hungry Eye in Chicago with the Vanguard Ensemble, founded by AACM drummer Ajaramu (Gerald Donavan). The jazz artist worked with Gene Ammons, Sonny Stitt and Lester Bowie before forming her own group Amina and Company. She has appeared at important piano rooms in New York City and has toured Germany, Belgium, Holland and Italy. Amina has conducted workshops for the "Artist in the Schools Program" and gives her all at annual women's festivals in New York and Kansas City. She appeared with the James Moody Quartet at Carnegie Hall during the 1982 Kool Jazz Festival in New York City. A few months earlier, the experienced musician recorded "Blythe Spirit" with Arthur Blythe. Her organ work on the selection "Just a Closer Walk With Thee," is reminiscent of her gospel roots and a joy to hear.

Italian-born Chessie Tanksley, in her mid-twenties, grew up in Munich, Germany, where she began playing professionally in 1977 with the George Morrison Big Band and George Greene's Hotline. The next two years were spent touring Germany with tenor sax player Erica Lindsay and other musicians. In 1980 she moved to New York and joined Melba Liston & Co. The thin brownette with pigtails appeared with Melba's group on the public television series, "Women in Jazz — A

Matter of Taste." The Erica Lindsay/Chessie Tanksley Quartet with Andy McCloud and Newman Baker appeared at The Dairy in Central Park in May of 1982.

Lillette Harris Jenkins is a veteran pianist, teacher and composer. Born one of nine children in New York City, she graduated from NYU and served four years in the Armed Forces Special Services. She's played major clubs aroud the world, appeared at Town Hall and Carnegie Hall and worked in films and television. Besides teaching in the New York public school system, she works as a music therapist in nursing homes. An album by the pianist was released in 1982 on the Masterpiece Sound Label. Her on-stage pianistic expertise provided an added dimension to the rollicking musical "One Mo' Time" which enjoyed a long run at the Village Gate.

Patrice Rushen is an accomplished keyboardist, composer and arranger who belies her small stature when she plays swinging piano. Born and raised in California, the young woman has been featured on several albums since 1974. She has worked with Melba Liston and Stanley Turrentine and is a regular at jazz festivals.

Among the many, many other fine women pianists playing jazz are Marilyn Crispell who performed on "Composition 98" (Hat Art), a double album that offers the same piece performed in two different settings, Esther Blue who works in Manhattan clubs, Ursula Oppens, Emme Kemp, Sumi Tonooka, Gretchen Ann Gould, Joan Wile, Bonita Sargent, Lisa Dean, Juli Homi and Silvia Zehn.

X

Present Progress, Future Expectations

"Consort not with a female musician, lest thou be taken in by her snares." (Book of Wisdom, c. 190 B.C.)

Women musicians today are aware that the ages have not eliminated sexism in the arts. Female pianists often encounter discrimination when trying to get hired or recorded, even before playing a note! Many remember being discouraged in some way by a male counterpart. Even successful women receiving good reviews haven't escaped the innuendos of discrimination. Reviews of pianist Lee Shaw from the 1960's illustrate the problem. Various critics expressed surprise that a "gorgeous redhead" and "good-looking doll" could perform admirably at the keyboard. They praised the musician who "plays like a man," whose "attack is masculine" and who "looks more like a housewife than a far-out musician."

Jazz has always been more available to men. They were frequently exposed to the music which spent its infancy on the streets, in brothels and on riverboats. As jazz developed, it was usually performed late at night in smoky clubs. Women who wished to play had to learn the subtleties and symbolism of the music in which male musicians were immersed from the beginning. There is also a theory that women in our culture have been hesitant to make an autobiographical statement in their music.

Today's consensus, however, is that more qualified women than ever before are entering the field and that with perserverance, they can realize their goals. Though earning a living in jazz is still difficult, they can experience those moments of transcendence that make it all worthwhile. They can fulfill their need, in singer-pianist Judy Powell's words, "to reach out and touch someone soul to soul."

Jazz has been a major influence on twentieth century music. But because of the manipulated musical tastes of the American public, jazz and jazz performers as a whole have not had it easy. However, the music has survived, and as more people are exposed to it through festivals and educational facilities, it will flourish.

The first important jazz festival was established by Mr. and Mrs. Louis Lorillard and produced by George Wein. The two-day affair took place in Newport, Rhode Island, in July of 1954. Eddie Condon appeared, along with Dizzy Gillespie and his quintet. Oscar Peterson's Trio played "Tenderly," and Gerry Mulligan's combo performed "The Lady Is a Tramp." When the annual event became too boisterous for Newport, it was moved to New York and later renamed the Kool Jazz Festival. By 1982, promoter George Wein presented jazz fests in 20 American cities under the Kool aegis. For 10 days, beginning June 25th, the metropolitan area of New York City hosted 1,000 musicians participating in 50 different concerts. The Kennedy Center in Washington, D.C., was taken over, with its four separate halls used for performances by top artists.

In Atlanta, San Diego, Philadelphia, Pittsburgh and Hampton, Virginia, jazz devotees absorbed the sounds of their favorite artists. Concerts at the Kool Jazz Festival and Heritage Fair in Orlando, Florida, featured George Shearing, Dave Brubeck, Ray Charles, Pete Fountain and other top names as well as local jazz groups. Four free concerts, one a late-night jam session, were held during the five-day fair.

During the early festival years, women musicians invited to participate were usually jazz vocalists (Billie Holiday, Mahalia Jackson, Ella Fitzgerald). Along the way, there were token appearances by women instrumentalists too prominent to be ignored. Women needed a stage of their own. While the first National Women's Music Festival (Champaign-Urbana, Illinois, 1974) was not profitable, it generated enough interest to repeat the event the following year. Woman's Soul Publishing Company published *Producing Concerts*, for women who needed information on the business aspects of putting together festivals. A few years later two enterprising Kansas City women, Carol Comer and Dianne Gregg, were driving back from the Wichita Jazz Festival. They lamented the fact that Kansas City, a cradle of jazz, had nothing comparable. Carol suggested organizing a *women's* jazz festival in their home town! The longer they drove, the less radical the concept seemed. When Carol and Dianne arrived home, they called Marian McPartland, who was delighted with the idea and eager to help.

The first Kansas City Women's Jazz Festival in 1978 was dedicated to the memory of Bettye Miller, a local jazz legend. Bettye was a superb pianist-vocalist whose death in 1977 at 49 saddened jazz fans everywhere. As the "Queen of Kansas City Jazz" for almost 30 years, Bettye performed both solo and with bassist Milt Abel, her husband. Her vivacious personality and versatile talents made her a consummate human being with many friends.

Talented women from all over the country participated in clinics, seminars and jam sessions during the festival. Their brilliant energetic musical offerings were eloquent proof that music has nothing to do with sex, race or ethnic background. Pianists Marian McPartland, Mary Lou Williams and Toshiko Akiyoshi were among the artists who performed. Mary Lou Williams, smiling and nodding approval at bassist Carline Ray and drummer Everett Brown, played part of "Mary Lou's Mass." She next performed several technically-astounding tunes, including "My Blue Heaven" and "Top Fly," and finished with an aural history of jazz, covering the terrain from blues to contemporary. The Akiyoshi/Tabackin Big Band demanded several encores after executing "Elusive Dream," "Kogun," and other compositions of its leader. "Studio J" starred Akiyoshi at the keyboard, reminding fans of the composer's pianistic skills. The McPartland trio displayed masterful dynamics and phrasing on originals "Ambience" and "Afterglow" as well as standard tunes. The popular pianist also conducted a clinic and performed with the festival All-Stars: trombonist Janice Robinson, guitarist Mary Osborne, bassist Lynn Milano, drummer Dottie Dodgion and flutist/saxophonist Mary Fettig Park. Singer Betty Carter, drummer Joe Morello, reedman Bunky Green, singer Carol Comer and jazz critic Leonard Feather were among those present to entertain and instruct.

Since its auspicious debut, the Kansas City Women's Jazz Festival becomes more successful every year, drawing top women (and men) musicians from around the country. Co-founders Comer's and Gregg's aims are to stimulate an interest in jazz in general and to create a demand for female jazz artists. The organization publishes a National Directory of Female Jazz Performers. An annual scholarship is awarded to a deserving student musician, and year-round clinics are provided in primary and secondary school systems as well as colleges.

The fifth annual Women's Jazz Festival in 1982 opened at the Folly Theatre with a solo concert by Blossom Dearie, whose intimate voice stylings and crystalline piano earned her four encores. The following evening the big-band invitational was held, featuring the All-City Women Students' Big Band, the University of Missouri at Kansas

City jazz band and the Indian Creek Junior High Jazz Band. Promising young musicians are aware of the importance of appearing at this prestigious event. The third evening's program consisted of the Top New Talent Concert, with combo contest winners Sweet Honey in the Rock, Tintomara, the Swing Sisters and Bougainvillea. The Music Hall was the setting for the main concert the final night. Nancy Wilson, Barbara Carroll and the Women Jazz Festival All-Stars concluded the festival with a rousing finale.

Veteran pianist Barbara Carroll's solo renditions of "I Love a Piano," "Spain" and other feats of harmonic virtuosity were outstanding. The All-Stars led by pianist Joanne Grauer were "the best of their kind in festival history," according to reviewer Terry Teachout of *The Kansas City Star*. Bassist Val Hammick, drummer Debbie Katz and sax players Ann Patterson and Lisa Gordanier consistently pleased the audience with their solos and ensemble work on their leader's original compositions. Joanne Grauer's keyboard brilliance was perfectly complimented by their presence. Songstress Nancy Wilson completed the program with a set of eclectic tunes delivered in her inimitable fashion.

In addition to the fine concerts, the festival offered jam sessions every day (some including well-known local jazzmen), and jazz critic Leonard Feather conducted a lecture and film presentation at a community college. A full five days of women's jazz came to a close with performers, producers and fans looking forward to the next festival.

Cobi Narita, executive director of the Universal Jazz Coalition in New York City, presented her fifth annual New York Women's Jazz Festival in June 1982. Pianist Esther Blue (with Kim Clarke on bass and Cindy Blackman on drums) led the "Smokin' Jam Session" on opening day. Shirley Horn, Joanne Brackeen, Patti Bown, Lady Byron, Michele Feldheim and Gloria Coleman appeared at different sites around the city with dozens of other women instrumentalists. Five days of performances, workshops, films and a seminar, "The Business of Jazz," concluded with a concert at St. Peter's Church, featuring Melba Liston and the 17-piece festival Big Band. Both Shirley Horn and Melba Liston were honored by the Universal Jazz Coalition.

In addition to producing an annual concert, Narita publishes a monthly calendar listing concerts, fundraisers and workshops which the Universal Jazz Coalition coordinates for established and emerging artist-participant members. Narita wrote in a recent newsletter, "Most of my work is with the young artists who find it so hard to get gigs — and if they get a gig, to get an audience. All of us, both player and appreciator, must work together to make sure that there will always be artists performing this music."

Other American cities have followed the examples of Kansas City and the Universal Jazz Coalition and initiated women's festivals of their own. Among them are Boston, San Francisco and Dearborn. Until there is no longer a need for women to promote themselves as competent musicians, these festivals will fill an obvious void.

The Kool Newport Jazz Festival in 1980 presented "Blues Is A Woman," a musical event co-produced by Rosetta Reitz and George Wein. Early classic blues singers and women composers were honored by a star-studded tribute at which pianist Sharon Freeman played three of Lil Hardin Armstrong's tunes. In 1981 "Women Blow Their Own Horns" displayed the talents of an All-Woman Jam Band, Willene Barton's quintet, Melba Liston & Company, and Dorothy Donegan. Rosetta Reitz is also a writer and record producer. Through her research, a wealth of early women's music is now available on her own label, Rosetta Records.

In 1982 a program on twentieth century women composers and lyricists was incorporated into the schedule, and female pianists including Patti Bown, Nina Sheldon, Amina Claudine Myers, Marian McPartland, Marie Marcus, Dorothy Donegan and Joanne Brackeen performed on different nights of the festival.

New York is a sanctuary for jazz which can be heard in such diverse settings as clubs, parks, concert halls, the Jazzmobile, St. John the Divine Church and St. Peter's Lutheran Church which provides a jazz ministry. Summerpier, a three-month series of free concerts by 14 different groups was introduced on Pier 16 on the East River in New York City. Jazz was the catalyst that brought thousands to the historic seaport district to visit the seaport museum and see the old sailing ships and counting houses. The 1981 concert turnout more than doubled that of 1980. Springtime of 1982 prompted six Manhattan clubs to offer jazz at noon or at twilight on Fridays, following the trend set by Condon's Hot Lunch six years earlier. Duos, trios and combos jam for the customers, who sometimes bring their own instruments from their offices to sit in. Pianist Amy Duncan was one of the musicians leading noontime jazz sessions.

Early summer brought jazz fests worldwide: the 16th Montreux International Festival in Switzerland, the North Sea Jazz Festival in The Hague, the Kongsberg Jazz Festival in Norway, the Nice Jazz Festival in the south of France and Jazz Festival East-West in Nurenberg, West Germany. There were also major concerts in Brazil and tours through Africa. The International Seminar on Jazz Education took place in Trossingen, West Germany. A bilingual jazz encyclopedia was published for the first time in the Soviet Union.

Since 1980, Detroit has been the American base of the Montreux Festival; it showcases the talents of native Detroit musicians for several days of jazz. Concerts are scattered over the downtown area, in churches, hotels, parks, museums and malls. Detroit pianists Bess Bonnier and Barry Harris were just two of the local talents who took to the stage recently during the daytime. Evening spotlights were reserved for name musicians like McCoy Tyner, Sarah Vaughan, Archie Shepp and Joanne Brackeen.

Two of Northern California's jazz events in 1982 were the 14th Annual Concord Jazz Festival and the 25th Monterey Jazz Festival, both headlining leading Jazz and blues players. Playboy's festival offered two days of jazz at the Hollywood Bowl. Sacramento caters to the "moldy figs" who prefer their jazz more traditional. In 1982, nearly 80 Dixieland bands from all over the world converged to participate in the Old Sacramento Dixieland Jubilee. The Wolf Trap Jazz Festival opened the season for the entire Wolf Trap schedule, which was relocated in a temporary facility after fire destroyed the main center. The Boston Globe Jazz Festival celebrated its 11th year in 1982 by featuring Dixieland, bebop, fusion and swing.

The midlands also offer many festivals that highlight jazz. Old-time quilting bees and displays of turn-of-the-century artifacts are accompanied by the hot licks of traditional jazz. Just one of many events in the Lone Star state, the Texas Jazz Festival in Corpus Christi celebrated its 22nd consecutive year. The first year of the Steamboat Days and Dixieland Jazz Festival on the Burlington, Iowa riverfront was 1963. A joyous week of steamboat races, trolley rides, fireworks and pageants closed with the Steamboat Ball. It's still going strong. In June of 1982, the six-day event featured three days of jazz along with sailboat races and hot air balloon rides. St. Louis presented a ragtime festival and Denver put on its Mile High Jazz Festival. New Orleans inaugurated the Jazz & Heritage Festival in 1970 with musicians playing to a small crowd in Congo Square. By 1982, a throng of 200,000 gathered to revel in nine days of music, fine cuisine and cultural appreciation. The Tulane Hot Jazz Classic offered jazz films, symposia on the art form, riverboat "jazz" cruises, a "Fingerbreaker" piano concert and a reunion of the city's pre-1940 jazz pioneers. Over 300 performances filled the bayou country with ragtime, Gospel, Cajun, bluegrass, traditional and contemporary jazz and march music of the brass bands. The informality of the times has helped introduce jazz to new fans who relax on blankets, stroll through art and craft exhibits and sample regional cuisines.

"Musical Memories," a show with a cast of 29, ran May through

October at the 1982 World's Fair in Knoxville, Tennessee. Fair visitors learned about America's musical heritage during the free presentation. Jazz was represented by the music of Scott Joplin, W.C. Handy, Duke Ellington, Count Basie and Louis Armstrong. On Broadway, the effervescent Fats Waller came to life in "Ain't Misbehavin'," a rollicking revue of 31 of his songs. After running 1,500 performances, it was nationally televised with the original cast to rave reviews. Jazz societies and foundations provide avenues for performers and aficionados who want to promote the cause of jazz.

A good omen for the future of jazz is the multitude of jazz festivals and summer music camps taking place on college campuses across the United States. Notre Dame's festivals, first introduced in 1958, play host to campus bands, soloists and performing groups, who are judged on the fine points of jazz. In 1966 the first Mobile Jazz Festival in Alabama welcomed collegiate jazz instrumentalists and vocalists who entered competitive events. Within a few years the festivals at Villanova, Columbia, the University of Cincinnati and the University of Kansas were in existence. The mid-1970's brought "A Week of Jazz" at Wichita State University. Noted artists monitored panel discussions and tutored students in theory, arranging and ear training. Clinics were conducted for combos and big bands. The University of Minnesota initiated annual non-competitive sessions for high school jazz bands with a guest artist judging performances. Visiting musicians also presided at clinics and soloed with the university jazz ensemble. Missouri State University held a similar annual competition for students who were invited to enter composition contests.

Increasingly good jazz education in many colleges has produced musicians of such high calibre that there have been instances where students are recruited as sidemen by professional road bands. Every time a professional jazz musician visits a school, the seeds of jazz are sown. The arts-in-education programs provided by International Art of Jazz and similar organizations are vital in introducing the profusion of varieties of jazz to young people. It has been proven that when young elementary school children learn to improvise on conventional musical instruments, they also improve their reading skills and math concepts. More girls than ever before have the opportunity to avail themselves to good jazz training. Those taking advantage of it are no longer considered lonely over-achievers. "I see a big difference at colleges over the past ten years." Marian McPartland attested. "There are more women in the bands and they are accepted whether playing trombone or alto. Sax sections have more women, sometimes first chair. There's a lot more interest in jazz, and the standards of playing are much higher."

Many all-female ensembles over the past few years include Calico, Sea Journey, About Time, Add Lib, Mam'selles, Quintess, Bonnie Janofsky/Roz Cron Big Band, Essence and Cheska. Maiden Voyage, an excellent all-woman band which has appeared on the "Tonight Show," first received critical acclaim at the Kansas City Women's Jazz Festival in 1980. Composer Mel Powell, who wrote for Benny Goodman's band in the 1930's, has written a full-scale composition for the band. Another group of women making an impact is Alive!, a quintet which has been together five years and recorded their second album during a performance in San Francisco. In response to a jazz critic's statement that jazz is "a peculiarly male music, [for which] most women lack the physical equipment—to say nothing of the poise," pianist Janet Small told Derek Richardson of *Jazz Times* (May 1982), "Kids growing up are not going to have those same prejudices because their moms are going to be out working." Marian McPartland envisions the day when, "No qualifying word is needed, like male or female."

As women have become more politically and economically aware, they have created a more positive future for themselves as artists. Today's women musicians are organized in their support for each other and have become proficient at networking. Their organizations sponsor radio programs and lecture/film series that stimulate interest in women jazz performers. Newsletters and directories are published, and recording companies started.

Jazz's embryonic melodies and rhythms first served to lighten the burden and monotony of daily tasks. For nearly a century, the family tree of jazz has extended its branches to welcome innovative refinements. Women keyboard artists have become proficient in every idiom of the music. Their knowledge, talent, creativity, resilience and dedication demand recognition. A career as a jazz artist no longer need be a chimera. As our indigenous American art form advances into its second century, more women than ever are prepared to embark on the odyssey.

Bibliography

Balliett, Whitney. *Improvising, 16 Musicians and Their Art*. New York: Oxford University Press, 1977.

Berendt, Joachim-Ernst. *Jazz: A Photo History*. New York: Schirmer, 1978.

Blesh, Rudi. *Combo USA: Eight Lives in Jazz*. Philadephia: Chilton, 1971.

Harriet, Janis. *They All Played Ragtime*. New York: Oak Publications, 1971.

Budds, Michael J. *Jazz in the Sixties*. Iowa City: University of Iowa Press, 1978.

Buerkle, Jack V. and Danny Barker. *Bourbon Street Black: The New Orleans Black Jazzmen*. New York: Oxford University Press, 1973.

Dance, Stanley. *The World of Duke Ellington*. New York: Scribner's, 1970.

————. *The World of Earl Hines*. New York: Scribner's, 1977.

Delaunay, Charles. *Hot Discography*. Paris: Commodore Record Co., 1938.

Dexter, Dave, Jr. *The Jazz Story from the '90s to the '60s*. Englewood Cliffs N.J.: Prentice-Hall, 1964.

Ellington, Edward Kennedy. *Music Is My Mistress*. New York: Doubleday, 1973.

Ellington, Mercer with Stanley Dance. *Duke Ellington in Person–An Intimate Memoir*. Boston: Houghton Mifflin, 1978.

Ewen, David. *All The Years of American Popular Music*. Englewood Cliffs N.J.: Prentice-Hall, 1977.

Feather, Leonard. *New Edition of Encyclopedia of Jazz*. New York: Horizon Press, 1960.

————, and Ira Gitler. *The Encyclopedia of Jazz in the Seventies*. New York: Horizon Press, 1976.

Gammon, Peter. *Scott Joplin and the Ragtime Era.* New York: St. Martin's Press, 1975.

Gitler, Ira. *Jazz Masters of the Forties.* New York: Collier-Macmillan, 1966.

Gottlieb, William P. *The Golden Age of Jazz.* New York: Simon & Schuster, 1979.

Handy, D. Antoinette. *Black Women in American Bands and Orchestras.* Metuchen, N.J.: Scarecrow Press, 1981.

Handy, W.C. *Blues; An Anthology.* New York: Macmillian, 1926.

Hentoff, Nat, and Albert J. McCarthy, eds. *Jazz.* New York: Rinehart, 1959.

Keepnews, Orrin, and Bill Grauer, Jr. *A Pictorial History of Jazz.* New York: Crown, 1961.

Kleiman, Carol. *Women's Networks; The Complete Guide to Getting a Better Job, Advancing Your Career, and Feeling Great As a Woman, Through Networking.* New York: Lippincott & Crowell, 1980.

Lyons, Len. *The 101 Best Jazz Albums: A History of Jazz on Records.* New York: William Morrow, 1980.

Meyer, Robert, Jr. *Festivals USA and Canada.* New York: Ives Washburn, 1970.

Panassie, Hugues, and Madeleine Gautier. *Guide to Jazz.* Boston: Houghton Mifflin, 1956.

Partnow, Elaine, ed. *The Quotable Woman (1800-1975).* Los Angeles: Corwin Books, 1977.

Russell, Ross. *Jazz Style in Kansas City and the Southwest.* Berkeley: University of California Press, 1971.

Shapiro, Nat, ed. *An Encyclopedia of Quotations About Music.* Garden City, N.Y.: Doubleday, 1978.

_____, and Nat Hentoff, eds. *Hear Me Talkin' to Ya.* New York: Dover Publications, 1955.

_____, and _____. *The Jazz Makers.* New York: Rinehart, 1957.

Shaw, Arnold. *52nd Street: The Street of Jazz.* New York: Da Capo Press, 1977.

_____. *The Street That Never Slept: New York's Fabled 52nd Street.* New York: Coward, McCann & Geoghegan, 1971.

Short, Bobby. *Black and White Baby.* New York: Dodd Mead, 1971.

Southern, Eileen. *The Music of Black Americans.* New York: W.W. Norton, 1971.

Stewart-Baxter, Derrick. *Ma Rainey and the Classic Blues Singers.* New York: Stein & Day, 1970.

Ullman, Michael. *Jazz Lives: Portraits in Words and Pictures.* Washington, D.C.: New Republic Books, 1980.

Walton, Ortiz M. *Music: Black, White & Blue.* New York: William Morrow & Co., 1972.

Wasserman, Paul, ed. *Festivals Sourcebook.* Detroit: Gale Research, 1977.

Weiser, Marjorie P.K., and Jean S. Arbiter. *Womanlist.* New York: Atheneum, 1981.

Williams, Martin T. *Jazz Master of New Orleans.* New York: Macmillian, 1967.

Wilmer, Valerie. *As Serious As Your Life: The Story of the New Jazz.* Westport, Conn.: Lawrence Hill, 1977.

Index

Able, Milt 168
Ables, Charles 163
Adams, Dolly 10
Adams, Pepper 133, 152
Adderly, Cannonball 113, 144
Ailey, Alvin 44
Ajaramu (Gerald Donovan) 164
Akiyoshi, Toshiko 93–94, 108, 168
Alexis, Richard 19
Allen, Henry 53
Allen, Jap 53
Allen, Steve 67, 124
Ammons, Gene 164
Anderson, Louella 7, 52
Anderson, Tom 10
Ann-Margret 145
Anthony, Ray 148
Armstrong, Irene 7, 56, 60–61
Armstrong, Lil Hardin 3, 22–30, 52, 100, 170
Armstrong, Louis 3, 10, 16, 22, 24, 25, 26, 27, 29, 30, 38, 42, 47, 53, 60, 133, 172
Asch, Moe 48
Atkinson, Brooks 75
Austin, Lovie 3, 8, 34, 47

Bailey, Buster 29
Baker, Harold "Shorty" 37, 39
Baker, Josephine 93
Baker, Newman 165
Ball, James 143
Balliett, Whitney 31
Barkedale, Everett 53
Barnes, Clive 44
Barnes, Paul 20
Barrett, Sweet Emma 11, 12, 15–19
Barron, Kenny 143

Bart, Wilhelmina 11
Barton, Willene 152, 164, 170
Basie, Count 6, 37, 55, 56, 57, 58, 79, 85, 131, 142, 146, 161, 172
Beatles, The 159
Bechet, Sidney 3
Beck, Florida 13
Beiderbecke, Bix 25
Bell, Gertrude "Sweety" 7
Bell, Iris 105–107
Bellson, Louis 83, 85, 121
Bennett, Tony 149
Berigan, Bunny 102
Berry, Bill 124
Berry, Chu 29
Bierach, Richie 130
Black, Ivy 56
Blackman, Cindy 169
Blake, Eubie 5, 9, 72
Blakey, Art 39, 47, 120, 129
Blakey, Evelyn 164
Blanchard, Kay 80
Bley, Carla 4, 72, 83, 108, 155–156
Bley, Paul 155
Bloom, Jane Ira 128
Blue, Esther 165, 169
Blythe, Arthur 164
Bodley, Bob 128
Bonnier, Bess 171
Booker, Beryl 48, 55
Boone, Lester 60
Boone, Pat 83
Borge, Victor 81
Boswell, Martha 10
Bowman, Dave 101
Bown, Edith 139
Bown, Patti 72, 137–142, 150, 153, 169, 170
Brackeen, Charles 119

Brackeen, Joanne 4, 72, 118–120, 126, 130, 131, 134, 145, 146, 147, 158, 169, 170, 171
Breckinbridge, Dardenelle 48, 55
Brignola, Nick 130, 133
Brown, Beth 108–109
Brown, Boyce 102
Brown, Cleo 56, 57–60, 68
Brown, "Dutchie" 58
Brown, Everett 58, 168
Brown, James 149
Brown, Joe 55
Brown, Laura 52
Brown, Mary Jane 111–112
Brown, Otis 108
Brown, Ray 90
Brubeck, Dave 58, 69, 88, 97, 167
Bryan, Paul 49
Burke, Joanne 49
Burley, Fletcher 33
Burley, Virginia 32
Burnside, Viola 48
Burson, Claudia 102–104
Burstyn, Ellen 82
Burt, Harry 161
Burton, Gary 155
Butler, Frank 90
Byrd, Charlie 61, 78
Byron, Lady 169

Cables, George 143
Calloway, Cab 38
Campbell, Francis 100–102
Campbell, Herb 101
Capers, Bobby 153
Capers, Valerie 4, 141, 150, 153–154
Carless, Dorothy 68
Carlyle, Una Mae 47, 53
Carmichael, Hoagy 25, 124
Carmichael, Judy 156–157
Carrere, Sidney 20
Carroll, Barbara 4, 72, 76–78, 91, 114, 124, 169
Carroll, Diahann 83
Carson, Norma 55, 127
Carter, Benny 53, 141
Carter, Betty 57, 93, 168
Carter, Jimmy and Rosalyn 48
Carter, Ron 143
Cassidy, David 83
Castle, JoAnn 67
Catlett, Sid 60
Cavanaugh, Dave 57

Cecchi, Al 83
Celestin, Oscar "Papa" 10, 12, 13, 15, 16, 19, 20
Chaligny, Paul 13
Charles, Ray 140, 167
Christian, Charlie 39
Citron, Mike 152
Clarke, Kenny 39
Clarke, Kim 169
Claxton, Roselle 37
Clayton, Jay 116
Clementi, Rio 126
Clooney, Betty & Rosemary 98
Cole, Buddy 91
Cole, Nat 76
Cole, Teddy 29
Coleman, Bill 48
Coleman, George 130, 133, 146
Coleman, Gloria 169
Coleman, Ornette 70
Collette, Buddy 85, 99
Collins, Joyce 88–90
Collins, Judy 149
Collins, Lee 8
Coltrane, Alice 55
Coltrane, John 56, 70
Comer, Carol 167, 168
Condon, Eddie 121, 167
Connor, Chris 106
Contino, Dick 98
Cook, Olivia (Lady Charlotte) 10
Coolidge, Rita 78
Coolman, Todd 142
Coon, Jackie 157
Corea, Chick 70, 72, 83, 108, 129
Corey, Ed 159
Cosby, Bill 89
Cox, Ida 7, 8, 13
Coy, Ann 54
Coy, Gene 54
Creath, Charlie 9
Creath, Marge 9
Crispell, Marilyn 165
Crosby, Bob 102
Crow, Bill 69
Curtis, Barbara Sutton 85–87

daCosta, Rae 68
Daily, Pete 62
Dance, Stanley 56
Davis, Eddie "Lockjaw" 56
Davis, Jean 152
Davis, Louise 152

Davis, Miles 39, 56, 163
Davis, Richard 124, 127, 143, 152
Davison, Wild Bill 62, 67
Dawson, Sid 85
Dean, Lisa 165
Dearie, Blossom 55, 168
DeJohnette, Jack 120
Delmenco, Lynn 81
dePorres, St. Martin 42
deRosa, Clem 70
Derry, June 91–92
Desdoumes, Mamie 6
Desmond, Cleo 54
Desvignes, Sidney 16
Dial, Auzie 9
Dickenson, Vic 57
Dickerson, Garvinia 53
DiPasqua, Mike 72, 130
Dockery, Wayne 152
Dodds, Baby 8, 27, 52, 60
Dodds, Johnny 24, 25, 27, 28, 60
Dodgion, Dottie 72, 168
Dominguez, Paul Jr. 10
Donegan, Dorothy 4, 92–93, 128, 170
Donnelly, Ted 37
Dorsey Brothers 38
Douglas, George 12
Duncan, Amy 170
Dureau, Eunice 81
Dutrey, Honor 24

Edison, Harry "Sweets" 146
Eisenhower, Dwight D. 20, 112
Eldridge, Roy 124, 157
Ellington, Daisy Kennedy 6
Ellington, Duke 6, 31, 33, 35, 38, 39, 42,
  45, 55, 56, 58, 68, 69, 70, 80, 86, 141,
  158, 172
Ellis, Don 155
Emery, Bob 65
Evans, Bill 72, 73, 83, 87, 108, 126, 129,
  131, 137, 151, 158, 159
Ewell, Don 100, 101

Fabry, Phyllis 114–115
Fair, Jane 152
Farmer, Art 155
Faye, Francis 54
Feather, Leonard 75, 85, 88, 94, 119,
  168, 169
Feather, Lorraine 83
Feldheim, Michele 169

Fields, Mercedes 10
Fields, W.C. 92
Fisk Jubilee Singers 6
Fitzgerald, Ella 93, 99, 131, 167
Flamm, Carol 115–117
Flanagan, Tommy 72, 134, 157
Floyd, Hugh 34
Floyd, Mamie 37, 38, 39
Foster, Abbey (Chinee) 20
Foster, Frank 143
Fountain, Pete 167
Francis, Albert 10
Franklin, Aretha 141
Franklin, Joe 133
Frazier, Cie 16, 18
Frazier, John 29
Freeman, Sharon 156, 170
French, Albert "Papa" 18, 20
Friedlander, John 63
Frishberg, Dave 55
Fuqua, Bonnie G. 104–105

Garland, Ed 24
Garland, Red 147
Garner, Erroll 40, 47, 115, 134, 137
Garson, Mike 83
Gassi, Christine 54
Geller, Elaine 56
Gershwin, George 75
Getz, Jane 145
Getz, Stan 120, 128
Gibbs, Terry 56, 83
Giddens, Gary 50
Gillespie, Dizzy 39, 40, 42, 43, 50, 76,
  93, 128, 153, 167
Gillespie, Lorraine 42
Glasby, Vivien 55
Glaser, Joe 38, 133
Glass, Phillip 108
Gomez, Eddie 120, 130
Gonsoulin, Bertha 52
Goodman, Benny 38, 40, 48, 69, 78, 173
Goodson, Edna 12
Goodson, Sadie 12, 13
Goodson, Wilhelmina Madison (*see* Bil-
  lie Pierce)
Gordon, Dexter 56, 119, 140
Gordanier, Lisa 169
Gottesman, Rose 40
Gould, Gretchen Ann 165
Granz, Norman 45, 93
Grauer, Joanne 81–85, 114, 169
Gray, Glen 38

Green, Bunky 168
Greenfield, Merriam 54
Gregg, Diane 167
Grey, Al 133
Grey, Noreen 134–136
Grigsby, Horace 103
Grove, Dick 83, 85
Guaraldi, Vince 88
Guinan, Tex 58
Gulchard, Al 85

Hackett, Bobby 67
Hale, Corky (Merrilyn Hecht) 147–150
Hall, Al 48
Hall, Minor 24
Hammick, Val 169
Hammond, John 39
Hampton, Lionel 105, 124
Hampton, Paula 152
Hancock, Herbie 129
Handy, W.C. 5, 172
Hanna, Roland 72, 151
Hardaway, Diamond Lil 53
Hardin, Lil (see Armstrong)
Harris, Barry 72, 171
Hart, Billy 53, 120, 163
Hart, Clarence 53
Heidt, Horace 98
Henderson, Bill 89
Henderson, Edmonia 8
Henderson, Fletcher 27, 28, 55
Henderson, Joe 120, 124
Henderson, Lil 9
Henderson, Skitch 123
Hentoff, Miranda 137
Hentoff, Nat 119
Hepple, Peter 150
Herzog, Arthur 60
Hightower, Lottie 52
Hightower, Willie 52
Hill, Chippie 7, 8
Hilton, Marge 160–163
Hines, Earl "Fatha" 6, 28, 33, 34, 52, 55,
    60, 61, 101
Hinton, Milt 121
Hipp, Jutta 56
Hodges, Johnny 124
Holden, Stephen 93
Holiday, Billie 40, 54, 60, 61, 131, 149,
    167
Holter, T. 35, 36
Homi, Julie 165
Hope, Bertha 164

Hope, Rob 159
Hopkins, Linda 7
Horn, Paul 83, 89, 99
Horn, Shirley 163, 169
Horowitz, Vladimir 2
Houston, Clint 120
Howard, Camille 55
Howard, Jack 32
Humes, Helen 124
Humphrey, Percy 16, 18
Humphrey, Willie 16, 18
Hunt, Pee Wee 101
Hunter, Alberta 7, 8
Hunter, Lloyd 53
Hutcherson, Bobby 119
Hutchinson, Dolly 7, 60
Hutchinson, Earl 60
Hutchinson, Pearl 7
Hutchinson, Theodosia 7
Hutton, Ina Ray 54, 63
Hyams, Margie 40
Hyman, Dick 7, 72

Ind, Peter 56

Jackson, Mahalia 167
Jackson, Marion 36, 142
Jaffe, Alan and Sandra 11
Jambor, Agi 108
James, Harry 148
Janofsky, Bonnie 81
Jansen, Nadine 98–100
Jarrett, Keith 83
Jarvis, Jane 121–125, 146, 147
Jefferson, Blind Lemon 7
Jenkins, Lillette Harris 165
Jenkins, Myrtle 54
Jesse, Joe 12, 13
Jobim, Antonio Carlos 109
Johnson, Bill 24
Johnson, Herb 100
Johnson, James P. 2, 5, 9, 33, 86, 88
Johnson, Marc 152
Johnson, Margaret 8, 54
Johnson, Pete 80
Jolly, Pete 83, 99
Jones, Betty Hall 79–81
Jones, Hank 72, 116
Jones, Jonah 29
Jones, Maggie 7
Jones, Quincy 83, 140, 141, 142
Jones, Sam 143, 145, 152

Joplin, Scott 172
Jordan, Duke 72
Josephson, Barney 45

Kapp, Jack 37
Katz, Debbie 169
Kaye, Mary 99
Keepnews, Orrin 18, 90
Kelly, Wynton 116
Kemp, Emme 165
Keppard, Freddie 29
Kessel, Barney 91
Killian, Lawrence 130
Kimball, Jeanette Salvant 11, 19–21
Kimball, Narvin 12, 16, 20
King, Jackie 54
King, Martin Luther, Jr. 141
King, Teddi 73
Kirk, Andy 34, 36, 39, 40, 91
Kirk, Roland 159
Kirkland, Kenny 143
Kitchings, Elden 61
Kopetz - Korf, Ada 73
Kral, Roy 72
Kristofferson, Kris 78
Krupa, Gene 85, 102
Kuhn, Steve 155

Ladnier, Tommy 8
Laine, Frankie 40
Lambert, Olaf 16
Lamond, Don 68
Langley, Otto 13
Larkins, Ellis 72
LaSpina, Steve 72
Lawson, Janet 152
Layton, "Preacher" Rollo 67, 101
Lee, George 57
Lee, Julia 56, 57
Lee, Peggy 70, 148
LeGrande, Michael 85
Leighton, Elaine 55
Leonard, Ada 63
Leonard, Harlan 54
Leonnig, Ron 87
Lewis, Joe 38
Lewis, John 72
Lewis, Marge 53
Lewis, Meade Lux 80
Lewis, Ramsey 53, 72
Leymarie, Isabelle 142–143
Liberace 149

Liberace, George 148
Liebman, Dave 130
Lind, Perry 143
Lindsay, Erica 164, 165
Lindsay, John 8
Liston, Melba 48, 164, 165, 169, 170
Litton, Lovell 107–108
Lloyd, Charles 119
London, Barbara 128, 157–160
Long, Gertrude 54
Long, Huey 29
Lorillard, Mrs. Louis 167
Louis, Joe 38
Lovett, Baby 57
Lunceford, Jimmie 35, 38
Lutcher, Nellie 53
Luther, Frank 143

Mabern, Harold 147
McCloud, Andy 165
McCrae, Carmen 61, 115
McGhee, Howard 133, 136
Mackay, Dave 89
McKenna, Dave 72, 87
McLawler, Sarah 48, 56
McManus, Jill 130, 141, 150–152, 153
MacMillan, Molly 125–126
McNeely, Jim 130
McPartland, Jimmy 68, 70
McPartland, Marian 3, 40, 46, 48, 49,
    50, 58, 63, 67–74, 85, 86, 87, 88, 90,
    99, 100, 103, 108, 111, 114, 115, 124,
    130, 131, 134, 141, 145, 156, 158, 167,
    168, 170, 172, 173
McShann, Jay 72
Magnusson, Bob 83
Manchester, Melissa 106
Mansfield, Charlotte 54
Mantler, Michael 155
Maples, Ida Mae 53
Marable, Fate 2
Marbuto, Ron 136
Marcus, Bill 67
Marcus, Marie 4, 65–67, 170
Marrero, John 20
Marrero, Simon 20
Marshall, Nancy 109–111
Martin, Freddie 148
Martin, Sara 7
Martin, Tony 149
Matlock, Mattie 62
Mayfield, Roland 36
Mboya, Tom 44

Mehus, Belle 96
Mercer, Johnny 70
Merjan, Barbara 128, 152
Michaelson, Julie and Maria 96
Michaelson, Lorna 95–98
Milano, Lynn 72, 152, 168
Miles, Lizzie 7
Milholland, Miss 33
Miller, Bettye 168
Miller, Glenn 139
Miller, Hal 143
Miller, Max and Jean 131
Miller, Mulgrew 143
Mili, Gjon 40
Milton, Roy 55, 79
Mingus, Charlie 128, 141, 152
Minor, Ethel 52
Mitchell, Edna 10
Mitchell, George 29
Mitchell, Margaret 5
Moed, Ed 116
Mojo 109
Moliere, Earnest and Paul 14
Monk, Thelonious 39, 73, 111, 134
Montague, Muriel 144
Mooney, Joe 161
Moore, Orvella 54
Moore, Reggie 130
Moorehead, Consuela Lee 126–128
Morello, Joe 69, 135, 168
Morton, Jelly Roll 3, 5, 8, 23, 33, 35, 52, 86
Mosier, Gladys 54
Mulligan, Gerry 149, 167
Mullins, Maizie 6
Murphy, Norman 85
Murphy, Rose 50, 54
Murphy, Turk 61
Myers, Amina Claudine 164, 170

Narita, Cobi 50, 160, 169
Nero, Peter 91, 115
Nicholas, "Wooden Joe" 13
Nichols, Red 57
Norvo, Red 57

O'Brien, Peter 43, 44, 45, 46, 48, 49
O'Bryant, Jimmy 8
Okari, Japhet 142
Oliver, King 2, 3, 10, 24, 25, 26, 27, 29, 52, 53
Olsen & Johnson 53

Oneppo, Martha 49
Oppens, Ursula 165
Orent, Milton 40
Ory, Kid 25, 28, 29
Osborne, Mary 40, 48, 55, 72, 168
Osmonds, The 83

Page, Hot Lips 57
Paige, Jewel 55
Palmer, Gladys 53
Palmer, Robert 153
Palmer, Singleton 85
Papp, Joseph 142
Park, Mary Fettig 168
Parker, Charlie 39, 43
Parker, Daisy 25
Patterson, Ann 169
Pavageau, Alcide "Slow Drag" 18
People, Joe 13
Perry, Bishop Harold 12
Peterson, Jeanne Arland 96
Peterson, Oscar 69, 72, 87, 93, 111, 126, 131, 133, 144, 167
Petit, Buddy 12, 13
Pichon, Walter "Fats" 20
Picou, Alphonse 3, 13
Pierce, Joseph LaCroix "DeDe" 11, 12, 13, 14, 15
Pierce, Wilhelmina "Billie" 11–15
Pilapil, Beatriz J. 103
Piron, Armand 16
Pizzarelli, Bucky 124
Poitier, Sidney 163
Polcer, Ed 121
Polinard, Patti 103
Pollack, Ben 36, 62, 91
Pollard, Terry 55
"Pork Chops" 14
Powell, Adam Clayton, Jr 41, 76
Powell, Benny 85
Powell, Bud 93, 108, 151
Powell, Eleanor 92
Powell, Judy 166
Powell, Mel 173
Powers, Ollie 27
Prater, Jane 54
Pratt, Lloyd 148
Preston, Billy 106
Previn, Andre 148
Prinze, Freddie 105

Quint, J.P. 110

Rachmaninoff, Sergei 2
Ragtime Mame 7
Rainey, Gertrude "Ma" 7, 8, 9, 34
Ray, Carline 56, 128, 168
Raymore, Victoria 54
Redd, Vi 72
Redman, Don 37
Reed, Rex 89, 98
Reitz, Rosetta 170
Remler, Emily 133
Rena, Kid 12, 13
Rice, Johnnie 54
Richards, Johnny 146
Richardson, Derk 173
Rickles, Don 99
Riser, Anna Mae 38
Ritchie, Clayton 101
Roane, Stephen 136
Roberts, Luckey 6
Robinchaux, John 16
Robinson, Bill "Bojangles" 35
Robinson, Janice 152, 168
Robinson, Jim 16, 18
Rodgers, Gene 54
Rogers, Shorty 98, 99
Rossen, Marguerite 55
Rotenberg, June 40, 54
Rousseau, August 20
Rowles, Jimmy 90
Rowles, Stacy 152
Rubenstein, Arthur 137, 139
Ruckert, Ann Johns 145
Rushen, Patrice 108, 165
Russell, William 12

Safranski, Eddie 68
St. Cyr, Johnny 28, 29
Sample, Joe 108
Sargent, Bonita 165
Sauls, Earl 136
Saville, Alphonse 127
Saxe, Sam 83
Sayles, Emmanuel 16, 18
Schroeder, Gene 101
Scott, Alma Lang 75
Scott, Hazel 4, 67, 68, 72, 75–76
Scott, Shirley 56, 103, 113
Scruggs, Willis 37, 49
Sea, Patricia 87–88
Severinson, Doc 123
Shank, Bud 83
Shapiro, Nat 140
Shaw, Elijah 85

Shaw, Lee 130–134, 166
Shaw, Stan 131, 133
Shearing, George 61, 73, 105, 115, 167
Sheldon, Nina 128–130, 170
Shepp, Archie 171
Sheppard, Ella 6
Short, Bobby 72
Silver, Horace 83
Simmons, Alberta 9
Simone, Nina 141, 149
Sims, Zoot 83
Singleton, Zutty 9, 53
Slim, Bumble Bee 54
Small, Janet 173
Smith, Bessie 7, 8, 12
Smith, Clara 7
Smith, Clarence 8
Smith, Clarence "Pinetop" 36, 58, 102
Smith, Edna 56
Smith, Eloise 6
Smith, Emma 53
Smith, Laura 7
Smith, Mamie 7
Smith, Paul 83
Smith, Stuff 99
Smith, Trixie 7
Smith, Willie "The Lion" 6, 86
Snow, Valaida 47, 55
Sokoloff, Vladimir 108
Souchon, Dr. Edmund 67
South, Eddie 123
Southern, Jeri 90
Spivey, Victoria 7, 52, 53
Stacy, Jess 123
Stafford, Jo 40
Staton, Dakota 61
Stein, Morrie 91
Stevens, Connie 83
Stevens, Phil 91
Stewart, Anna 19
Stewart, Slam 53
Stitt, Sonny 141, 164
Stobart, Kathy 48
Stoller, Mike 149
Story, Sidney 2
Strauss, Judy 112–114
Strayhorn, Billy 139
Streisand, Barbra 81
String Bean 8
Sullivan, Maxine 124
Sutton, Ralph 86, 101
Szabo, Gabor 83

Tabackin, Lew 94
Tanksley, Chessie 164, 165
Tate, Erskine 28
Tate, Grady 124
Tatum, Art 2, 38, 43, 55, 60, 76, 78,
  80, 87, 91, 92, 108, 111, 134, 147
Taylor, Billy 40, 50, 72, 143
Taylor, Cecil 48
Taylor, Lottie 10
Teachout, Terry 169
Teagarden, Charlie 6, 61, 63
Teagarden, Clois 6, 61, 63
Teagarden, Jack 6, 36, 61, 63
Teagarden, "Mama" 6, 61, 63
Teagarden, Norma 4, 6, 47, 56, 61–64,
  67, 86, 91, 99, 100, 101
Terkel, Studs 74
Terry, Clark 71, 124, 134
Thigpen, Ben 37
Thigpen, Ed 56

Thomas, Joe 29
Thuenen, Tommy 102
Tirro, Frank 46
Todd, Camilla 10
Tolles, Billy 140
Tomlin, Lily 83
Tonooka, Sumi 165
Torff, Brian 45, 143, 152
Torme, Mel 91, 149
Trance, Nancy 54
Truman, President Harry 57
Turrentine, Stanley 84, 165
Tyner, McCoy 108, 116, 129, 164, 171

Ulanov, Barry 42

Vaughan, Sarah 55, 126, 140, 171
Vaughn, Father Tom 83
Viola, Al 148

Wagner, Paul 75
Wallace, Sippie 7
Waller, Adeline Lockett 6
Waller, Edward 6
Waller, Thomas "Fats" 2, 6, 35, 53, 58,
  65, 67, 80, 86, 87, 88, 102, 111, 153,
  157, 171

Walton, Cedar 72
Washington, Dinah 140, 141
Waters, Ethel 7, 8, 60
Webster, Ben 57
Wein, George 45, 167, 169
Wells, Gertie 52
Wetzel, Bonnie 55
Wheeler, Dave 116
White, Ola 113
Whiteman, Paul 25, 40
Wicks, Patti 143–145
Wilbur, Bob 121
Wilder, Alec 70
Wile, Joan 165
Wilkinson, Don 103
Williams, Andy 83, 84
Williams, Edith 37, 54
Williams, Jessica Jennifer 164
Williams, John 35, 39, 46
Williams, Lucy 52
Williams, Mary Lou (Mary Elfrieda
  Scruggs) 3, 5, 31–51, 53, 54, 56, 61,
  65, 67, 68, 72, 80, 91, 103, 111, 124,
  127, 128, 134, 142, 168
Williams, Paul 83
Williams, Roger 85, 88
Wilson, Dick 37
Wilson, John S. 78, 135, 136, 141, 144,
  151, 153
Wilson, Nancy 169
Wilson, Teddy 54, 60, 72, 76, 80, 88,
  91, 104, 123
Wilson, Vi 81
Winburn, Anna Mae 54
Winding, Kai 99
Woods, Fr. Anthony 42, 43
Woods, Willie 13
Wright, John Cardinal 44
Wrightsman, Stan 91

"Yeah Man" 14
Young, Billie 52
Young, Emma D. 6
Young, Lester 52, 57
Young, Lisetta 52
Young, Ruby 55

Zehn, Silvia 165
Zurke, Bob 91